The SENIOR'S GOLF SCHOOL

The SENIOR'S GOLF SCHOOL

HOW I WENT FROM 28 TO SCRATCH AGED 70

JOHN YOUNGBLOOD

foulsham
LONDON • NEW YORK • TORONTO • SYDNEY

foulsham

The Publishing House, Bennetts Close, Cippenham, Slough, Berkshire, SL1 5AP, England

This book is dedicated to every person who has touched golf clubs and to those who plan to touch golf clubs in the future.

ISBN 0-572-02890-3

Copyright © 2003 W. Foulsham & Co. Ltd

Original edition published in USA by Price Stern Sloan Inc., Los Angeles, California copyright © John Youngblood

Back cover photograph © Eric Hepworth

Printed in Great Britain by St Edmundsbury Press, Bury St Edmunds, Suffolk

Acknowledgements

To Paul Azinger for his endorsement and for the photographs illustrating the book. I am proud of Paul's achievements during his golfing career, and of my work with him on this book. To Paul and his father, Ralph Azinger, for their additions and corrections, which improved the quality of the manuscript.

To Jerry Shelke, Director of Golf at Rolling Hills Golf Resort, Plantation, Florida. Jerry arranged for the photographs of Paul Azinger to be taken at Rolling Hills. To Tom Thurston, Apogee Photographic, Inc., Fort Lauderdale, Florida. Tom supplied other photographs of Paul for the book.

To Marlene Moran, Fort Lauderdale, Florida, for superior typing and diligent work in preparing the manuscript.

About the Author

John Youngblood, a business executive, had played golf for 30 years, playing to a 4 handicap in his earlier years. Then a back injury stopped all his golf activity for five years. Starting golf again, Youngblood found he had a mental block against turning and a problem breaking 100. He arranged a series of lessons with a PGA teaching professional; but he couldn't break the mental block, so the lessons were unsuccessful. Believing that playing and practice could produce results, he played twice a week and finally attained a 10 handicap but became stuck there.

Through extensive research on all golf swings, he developed the Ultimate Swing Fundamentals. Deciding to have a final try to rebuild his game, he started with putting, developing a programme of learning and practice. This was so successful that he developed a similar programme for every golf club in the set. He realised that each golf stroke is only slightly longer than the previous stroke. The programmes developed with each club became the Step-by-step Learning and Practice Programme, which provides the backbone of the instruction in this book.

After progressing through the game with each club, Youngblood's handicap began to drop, and finally the great day arrived when it became scratch. Discussing this programme with senior golf professional, George Lumsden, he suggested that this system was foolproof and that it should be made available to other golfers in a book. Thus *The Senior's Golf School* was born.

CONTENTS

FOREWORD

The purpose of this book – and its proven success – is to provide sound instruction to help you improve your golf-ball striking ability and reduce your scores. John Youngblood's Ultimate Golf Swing Fundamentals and Step-by-step Learning and Practice Programme describe a natural progression of the skills required to get better at golf. This book is easy to read and understand. If followed, this plan will help just about anyone get his or her handicap down and enjoy the game more.

In the photographs, I have to tried to demonstrate the proper execution of the principles he proposes. I hope they will help to bring the written word to life.

Becoming a better golfer requires plenty of hard work, but if you have the desire, the book will serve as a good guide. Follow it closely and I'm sure that as your scores get lower, golf will be a lot more fun for you. After all, that's what the game of golf is intended to be – fun!

Paul Azinger
PGA Professional Golfer

PREFACE

The Senior's Golf School was written by a duffer for duffers who are stalemated at scores between 90 and 100 and who want very much to reduce their handicaps. This book is also written for those of all ages who want to learn to play golf. Since I had retired when I developed and implemented the programme, it follows that it offers an ideal course for others of more mature years, who want to spend time improving their game. But it's equally useful for anyone who is just starting out in the game.

The principles and practice have been thoroughly researched and the book has been written to serve as a textbook for learning golf and its benefits. Set yourself a goal and use the Ultimate Golf Swing Fundamentals and the Step-by-step Learning and Practice Programme to accomplish this goals.

The lifelong benefits of the game of golf are worth the hard work that goes into it. And the sense of satisfaction you can gain from improving your scores makes it better still.

The author and major PGA winner, Paul Azinger, at Rolling Hills Golf Resort.

INTRODUCTION

'If I played golf like John, I would give up the game.' Those words came like a clap of thunder from some tall bushes, where I had pushed by drive on the third hole. I recognised the voice as that of an elder in our church, and what made it so incredible was the fact that his game, with a 28 handicap, was no better than mine. I was stunned and hurt by those words, for I deeply respected the man who spoke them. I little realised the profound impact those words would have on my future actions in golf.

I was president of Plantation Golf Club that year and we were playing our last tournament of the season. The Parkway Golf Association, as we call our group, are golfers from the Parkway Christian Church, who play in a tournament once a month. Prizes are awarded for the Longest Drive, Nearest the Pin, Low Gross and Low Net. The golfers who win the most in monthly tournaments received an annual trophy at the final banquet at the end of the season. I had won Nearest the Pin the preceding year. We finished the last tournament, and that evening we gathered at a plush restaurant for our banquet.

After the meal, I signalled for silence and the awarding of the annual trophies began. The Longest Drive, Nearest the Pin and Low Gross were awarded by Ray, an elder in the church and a good friend of mine. The elder who spoke those words on the golf course that day didn't win a trophy that night. It was with some satisfaction that I took home the trophy for Low Net. However, my 28 handicap made the victory somewhat hollow.

That night we also elected new officers. I was nominated for a second term, and in the nominating speech I was told that I was the best president they had ever had. I refused the nomination, saying that I either had to give more attention to my game or give it up. These words were to underpin my struggle to play decent golf at a 4 handicap again. I had become a senior citizen that year, but luckily I had kept myself in good physical shape with a good balanced diet and regular exercise. I decided to rest over the Christmas holiday and then begin my assault on lowering my handicap.

I decided to seek the services of a PGA professional. David Anderson was the resident pro at the Jacaranda Country Club in Plantation, Florida. We discussed my problems, and I told him that my back injury had recovered through physical therapy, but that I had been left with a mental block against turning my hips. Dave felt that we could overcome this problem and we arranged for ten lessons.

I started with great anticipation. David checked my grip and stance and said they were good. We worked on my backswing, downswing, impact and followthrough. Each lesson consisted of a warm-up with the 5 iron, then work with the short irons and later the long irons. Towards the last lesson, we worked with the woods and, for some reason, I relaxed with the woods and each shot was almost perfect. Dave said: 'You hit beautiful wood shots. Now just practise the irons until you can hit them the same way.'

The irons gave me trouble. When I changed clubs, it took several tries to start hitting good shots. Dave said that my swing was 'basically good' and thought that practice was the answer. But I wasn't completely satisfied. I was eager to play good golf again, and the iron shots worried me a great deal.

I decided to remedy the situation by playing twice a week. I soon learned that the benefit of regular play was to transfer my attention to playing the course and solving the course problems. I began to aim my shots to areas where the following shots could be easier. Ever so gradually, my handicap began to drop. I broke 90, then settled around 83, where I became bogged down. I wondered if I would ever break 80 again.

To play twice a week meant that I had to get up early and be the first player to register in order to fill in with a group that had a missing player. I usually made a tee-off with one of the first three groups. I played just as the sun rose, and the first nine holes were wet, so I had to learn to play a wet weather game. I played with all kinds of golfers – young and old – with handicaps from scratch to 28. Many times the other players were surprised at my good wood shots but mediocre iron shots.

It was while I was filling in that I first played with fellow golfer, Ty Weller. He shot 83, and invited me to lunch with him after our round. Ty and I became friends and we decided to play early every Thursday and have lunch afterwards. I marvelled at Ty's courage. He had phlebitis, an inflammation of the veins, and had to wrap his legs before playing golf. Ty hit a lot of good shots and I found it nip and tuck to beat him about every other round. We were both stuck around 83. Ty and I ended our association after he took a long vacation to North Carolina. I told him I had decided not to play on a regular basis during the forthcoming season.

I became despondent about my game. With all the hard playing I had done, I felt my handicap should be lower. I thought about my situation long and hard, and I began to say to myself: 'Maybe it is time for me to quit the game.'

I continued to exercise and decided to develop golf exercises and work them into my regular routine. I posed in all positions with a 5 iron before a full-length mirror. One day, as I swung the club from the stance to the backswing position, I noticed my right knee quivering and moving back and forth. I realised at once that this accounted for many errant shots. The right leg must stay flexed but firm and not move during the backswing. Through practice exercises, I developed control of my right knee to cure this problem. To help my turn, I began to exercise, turning around my spine. I became good at this and eventually began to shift my weight naturally and at the proper time.

I wanted to keep my game going too, so I decided to play once a week and to practise in the middle of the week. I concentrated on turning and on keeping my right leg still. My scores began to drop. I broke 80, and 79 became my new goal each time I played. Now encouraged, I decided to make a final assault on the game of golf. Little did I know it at the time, but this decision was to lead to the development of the Ultimate Golf Swing Fundamentals and the Step-by-step Learning and Practice Programme that form the basis of this book.

CHAPTER 1
HOW THE PROGRAMME DEVELOPED

My determination to change my fortunes in the game were to be more far-reaching than I had ever envisaged.

During my working years in business, I had supervised a lot of research with a team of research staff. Those methods would stand me in good stead now as I realised I could utilise them to examine the elements of a successful golf swing. I decided to study every prominent golfer who every played the game and list the things common to most of them. This study was to cover golf from its inception. My vision was clear. Galloping out of all these statistics would come the Ultimate Golf Swing Fundamentals, distilled from the essence of every golf swing and shot by pro and amateur alike. This is precisely what I did. I constructed spreadsheets, researched golfers and selected the fundamentals common to most golfers. From this data came the Ultimate Golf Swing Fundamentals.

The Ultimate Golf Swing Fundamentals

These were the principles I established from all this comprehensive research. I tested these principles by playing once each week and practising for five hours in the middle of each week. I'll go into more detail, fully illustrated in Chapter 5.

The Grip

The Vardon grip is the most commonly used golf grip. The key in this grip is that the little finger of the right hand should overlap the index finger of the left hand.

The Address for the Drive

1 Keep your heels shoulder-width apart.

2 Turn your front (left) foot out to ten o'clock.

3 Straighten your right foot or keep it turned to one o'clock.

4 Flex your knees.

5 Keep your elbows close together.

6 Keep your arms straight but not rigid.

7 Straighten your left arm.

8 Keep your right arm soft.

9 Bend forwards from the hips until your weight is on the balls of your feet.

The Backswing

Move the triangle of your shoulders, arms and hands – co-ordinated with your hips – straight back from the ball past your right foot and continue upwards to a full backswing. Your wrists will cock naturally above your head. Your shoulders will turn fully and your back will face the target. Your hips also turn. The club will point over the right shoulder towards the target. The club can then be taken back to the horizontal.

The Downswing

The downswing begins by turning your left hip to the left, which causes your left heel to lower and your weight to begin to transfer to your left leg. This drops the triangle of your shoulders, arms and hands towards your waist and your right foot, as your arms and hands move into the hitting area, below your waist. Your left hand will be guiding and your right hand will be ready to smash the ball.

The Impact

The swing is down and through the ball. The clubhead contacts the ball slightly on the upswing, sweeping the ball off the tee. Your body position at impact is about the same as it was at the address.

The Followthrough

The swing should be done around a steady spine. The address posture stays the same throughout the swing. As the triangle of your shoulders, arms and hands moves downwards through impact, your right arm straightens and both arms are extended towards the target. Your weight transfers to your left foot and pulls your body round to face the target. Your left arm breaks and the club then finishes high over your left shoulder.

Practising and Moving On

After only one month on this programme, my handicap dropped to 4 again and at long last my full confidence was regained. There's nothing like seeing real progress to spur you on to even more success. I knew that I had made the right decision to give my golf one more shot and felt encouraged to move on to the next stage.

How I Began my Unique Programme

Encouraged by my success with the Ultimate Golf Swing Fundamentals, I decided to develop an ultimate practice and learning programme so I could combine the two and put them into practice.

I realised that putting was the foundation of good golf. I thought of a system to dramatise this for the player who wanted to improve his or her handicap, and which would also be serviceable for a beginner learning the basic skills of golf.

I thought about the 14 clubs used to play the game – and one day it came to me! I said: 'The putt is the basic stroke, and the stroke for a chip is only slightly longer than the putt. The same is true as we go up the ladder of the clubs.' Suddenly, the step-by-step idea was born and I refined it into my Step-by-step Learning and Practice Programme. With the Ultimate Golf Swing Fundamentals, this forms the foundation for all the instructions and information that follow in this book.

The step-by-step programme means exactly that. The programme begins with putting, and you should not take the next step up the staircase to chipping until you have mastered every putting stroke and eliminated every putting problem. This follows right the way up the staircase. It is essential that you practise until you have perfected every shot possible with each of the clubs listed on each step before moving to the step above. Skipping steps will destroy the programme because learning each step to perfection forms the foundation to the work on the next step. Diligence in executing this programme will produce just one thing: it will make a better golfer out of you!

I attacked the step-by-step programme with a vengeance. I was determined to use it to perfect every possible shot with each club needed to play scratch golf. In the beautiful surroundings of the

The Step-by-step Learning and Practice Programme

Jacaranda Country Club, I began to practise for five hours every Wednesday, on the putting green and the driving range, playing a round once a week. This is how I progressed. For those of you who are retired, this is not a great commitment of time when the rewards are so great. Of course, if you can only spare a shorter time for your practice, the improvements may take a little longer, but they will still be gradual and remarkable.

Step 1: Putting

My work in putting was set up on the 36-hole practice green at the Jacaranda Country Club. Before each session, I would check my grip – the overlapping grip – and my stance. My heels are 10 in/25 cm apart. My knees are flexed and I bend forwards from the hips until my eyes are directly over the ball. I play the ball just off my left heel, placing my putter squarely behind the ball. I hit a few warm-up putts, both long and short, then I am ready to practise.

I start by placing balls in a circle 2½ ft/76 cm from the hole. I practise these putts until I am able to drop them all perfectly. I then move the balls to 10 ft/3 metres from the hole and practise until all the balls drop into the hole.

I use the same technique to putt from 25 ft/7.6 metres. I practise until I drop 50 per cent and the rest come within 6 in/15 cm of the hole. I do the same from 50 ft/15 metres, but I practise until all puts are within a 12 in/30 cm circle around the hole. This is the way I practise on the green.

I go to the fringe of the green and, moving away from its surface, I place balls up to 30 ft/9 metres from the hole. I keep practising until I can drop the closer putts and leave the longer putts about 12 in/30 cm from the hole. I then move to a sand trap with no lip and hit balls until I can putt from the sand to within 12 in/30 cm of the hole.

In all putts, I move the club with the triangle of my arms, shoulders and hands, keeping the grip just firm enough to have good control of the putter. I notice the contours of the green and how they will affect the movement of the ball. I putt to the high side of the hole so the ball will have a chance to fall, trying to put rhythm into the swing so that all the putts are smooth. I practise this putting procedure for five days until I have mastered it. Only then do I move up to the next step on the staircase.

After each period on the practice green, I move to the driving range to work on shots, beginning with the sand wedge. These are high, lofting shots. I hit five balls in succession to land within a 3 ft/90 cm circle around the hole on the green. I use the Ultimate Golf Swing Fundamentals with each club listed in the step-by-step programme.

Step 2: Chipping

The putting grip can also be used for chip shots. The chip shot swing is a natural extension of the putting stroke. My chipping stance is slightly open and slightly more upright. My heels are 5 in/12 cm apart and my head higher. The ball is placed at the centre of my stance. I use the 5, 6 and 7 irons for chip shots. My triangle moves the club back and through the ball. There is no wrist break in the chipping stroke and my left arm is kept straight. My right elbow is kept close to my right hip. I let the club lift the ball by using a slight descending stroke.

I hit chip shots at varying distances, from 100 ft/ 30 metres from the fairway on into the pin. The ball should land on the green and roll to the hole. I practise until proficiency is such that only an uphill tap-in is left at the hole. I practise chip shots from the fringe and from sand traps with no lips. I practise all chip shots to drop in the hole or have a 6 in/15 cm tap-in. I allow for the way the contour of the green affects the ball. On the driving range, I am still working with pitch shots.

Step 3: Short Pitch Shots

For short pitch shots, I use the Vardon, or overlapping grip. My stance for the short pitch shot has knees flexed and hands ahead of the ball; my stance is open (feet, hips and shoulders aligned left of the target), with my heels 10 in/25 cm apart. My weight is slightly on the left foot. The ball is played a little ahead of my right heel. There is little body movement in short pitch shots. I use the pendulum swing and stroke the ball smoothly to the target. The backswing is shorter than the forward swing; my followthrough will be lower. I visualise the target before swinging, and think 'target' when I swing.

I hit short pitch shots over bunkers, rough terrain or obstacles where a chip shot is not feasible. I consider the contour of the green, and I practise all short pitch shots until a short uphill tap-in at the hole is left. The irons for these shots are the 7, 8, 9 irons or wedge. I use the short pitch shot from the fairway 50 yards/45 metres into the pin. A waist-high backswing will move the ball 40 yards/36 metres, while a one-third backswing will move the ball 25 yards/22 metres with an 8 iron. The short irons are the clubs I use on the driving range. The short irons are as follows: sand wedge, pitching wedge, 9 iron and 8 iron.

Step 4: Pitch Shots

Pitch shots are high, lofting shots and are made from 100 yards/91 metres to 50 yards/45 metres from the green. These shots are made with the 6, 7, 8 and 9 irons.

My motion in pitch shots relates to the motion of tossing a tennis ball underhand. My full backswing reaches just above my waist. My wrists hinge slightly and my weight shifts slightly to my left foot. My followthrough is slightly longer than the backswing.

My stance is open, with feet 10 in/25 cm apart; knees flexed; weight slightly over the left foot; my hands are ahead of the ball. My eyes are over the ball, which is placed ahead of the right heel, towards the centre of my stance.

My triangle moves the club back until the wrists start to cock, just past hip height. My triangle is swing down on the same path and through the ball to my followthrough. I keep my hands ahead of the clubhead in the downswing. Keeping body movements to a minimum, I aim all pitch shots to the pin. I practise by hitting five balls in succession until I can place all five in a cluster 3 ft/90 cm from the hole.

Step 5: The Short Irons

Short irons are precision clubs for pitch shots, full shots, shots from rough, high grass, greenside and fairway bunkers. A full swing three-quarters high is necessary to obtain the distances listed below. My stance is open with heels 10 in/25 cm apart. I play the ball at centre between the feet. My hands are ahead of the ball and my weight is favouring the left foot. My knees are flexed and I bend forwards from the hips.

My average distances with the short irons are:

- **Sand wedge:** 75 yards/68 metres
- **Pitching wedge:** 105 yards/96 metres
- **9 iron:** 115 yards/105 metres
- **8 iron:** 125 yards/114 metres
- **7 iron:** 130 yards/119 metres

In the backswing, I move the triangle straight back from the ball past the right foot upwards until my wrists cock just at shoulder height. My club will point over my right shoulder towards the target. I start the downswing by turning my left hip to the left, which pulls the triangle down. My head stays behind the ball as my triangle moves into the impact area and down and through to a natural, high followthrough.

I hit five balls in succession with each short iron until I can land all five shots in a cluster 3 ft/90 cm from the pin. I also practise fade and draw shots (working the ball from left to right and vice versa) in the same way. At each practice session preceding work on the driving range, I practise putting, chipping and short pitch shots. I am, therefore, already warmed up when I start to practise on the driving range. This is important as you should always warm up before driving practice or a game.

Step 6: The Middle Irons

My average distances with the middle irons are:

- **6 iron:** 140 yards/128 metres
- **5 iron:** 155 yards/142 metres
- **4 iron:** 165 yards/151 metres

I use the middle irons for full shots from the fairway to the green. They are also used for long bunker shots. My swing with the middle iron is compact, the grip firm, the backswing short – just to shoulder height. The stance is more upright, as the length of the club dictates. My stance for the middle irons is open; my heels 14 in/35 cm apart; weight on the left foot and hands ahead of the ball. The ball is played back from the centre of my stance. My knees are flexed and I bend forwards from my hips.

The club must be swung smoothly, counting 'one and two'. The triangle moves straight back past the right foot and continues upwards to a three-quarter backswing. The wrists cock naturally and the club points over my right shoulder towards the target.

I turn my hips to the left to begin the downswing. This also moves my hands and arms downwards towards the waist, and my weight transfers to the left leg. The triangle continues downwards past the right knee into the hitting area. The left hand guides the club and the right hand smashes the ball at impact. My body position at impact is about the same as it was at the address. The swing continues past impact on out towards the target. My right arm straightens and my left arm folds into a natural followthrough with my body facing the target.

I hit the middle irons by determining the distance for which I can use each club. I hit five balls until I can hit them close together on the driving range. I do the same practice with each club. I also work on fading and drawing the ball.

Step 7: The Long Irons

My average distances with the long irons are:

- **3 iron:** 175 yards/160 metres
- **2 iron:** 185 yards/169 metres

The long irons are needed for long shots from the fairway. I make certain that the longer backswing and forward swing are rhythmic and smooth.

The swing with the long irons is a sweeping swing when the lie of the ball is good. Tight lies require a downward stroke, striking the ball first and then taking the turf. My hands reach no higher than the top of the shoulder in the backswing. My stance for the long irons is square; my heels are 18 in/46 cm apart; my weight is slightly on the left foot. My hands are slightly ahead of the ball which is placed 4 in/10 cm back from my left heel. My knees are flexed and I bend from the hips.

The swing with the long irons begins with the left arm straight and the right arm soft. I move the triangle back from the ball, past the right foot, then continue upwards to a full backswing with the wrists cocked above my shoulder level. My shoulders turn fully with my back to the target. The club will point over my right shoulder towards the target.

The downswing begins with my hips turning to the left. This drops the triangle towards the waist and begins the transfer of my weight to the left foot. The triangle continues into the hitting area, the left hand guiding and the right hand ready to smash the ball at impact. The swing is down and through the ball with turf taken after the hit. The swing continues through impact on out towards the target. My right arm straightens and the left arm folds into a natural followthrough with the body facing towards the target.

I hit long irons smoothly and with good timing, letting the club do the work. I hit the long irons on the driving range, hitting five balls in succession until I can land them close together on the range. I hit the same number of balls with each long iron club. I hit both fades and draws with the long irons. I swing long irons with the same force as I use with the middle irons. Rhythm and good timing result in good and easy shots.

Step 8: The Fairway Woods

The fairway woods and their distances are:

- **5 wood:** 185 yards/169 metres
- **4 wood:** 200 yards/183 metres
- **3 wood:** 220 yards/201 metres

I use the fairway woods for tee shots and for good lies on the fairway. I use the sweeping stroke from good lies and the downward stroke for tight lies. I use the 5 wood from the rough if the lie is good enough.

My stance with the fairway woods is square; heels 20 in/50 cm apart; weight slightly on the target foot. The ball is placed 2 in/5 cm back from my left heel. My hands are slightly ahead of the ball. My knees are flexed and I bend forwards from the hips.

The swing begins with the left arm straight and the right arm soft. I move the triangle straight back from the ball past my right foot and continue upwards to a full backswing. My wrists have cocked naturally near the top of my head. The club points over my right shoulder towards the target. The downswing begins when I turn my hips to the left, which causes the triangle to drop towards my waist. My weight begins to transfer to the left foot. My body position stays steady as my triangle moves into the hitting area, with the left hand guiding and the right hand ready to smash the ball at impact.

My swing is down and through the ball. The swing continues through impact; my right arm straightens and my left arm folds into a natural, high followthrough. The swing has rotated around my spine as my spine stays in exactly the same position throughout the swing.

For a good lie on the fairway, I use a sweeping stroke and for tight lies I use a downward stroke, taking turf after striking the ball. I practise fairway woods on the driving range. I hit five balls until I can cluster them close together on the range. I practise straight shots first, then work the say way, perfecting fades and draws, with all the fairway woods.

Step 9: The Driver

Balance and relaxation are important in working with the driver. My stance is slightly closed (feet, hips and shoulders pointing slightly right of the target), with the heels a shoulder-width apart. The ball is placed 1 in/2.5 cm back from the left heel. My hands are slightly behind the ball; my knees are flexed and I bend forwards from the hips until my arms hang free.

My backswing begins with my left arm straight and my right arm soft. I move the triangle straight back from the ball past the rear foot and continue upwards to a full backswing with my wrists cocked naturally above my head. My shoulders turn fully with my back towards the target. The driver will point over my right shoulder at the target.

My downswing begins by turning my hips to the left, which drops the triangle towards my waist. My weight also begins to transfer to my left leg. The swing continues as my triangle moves my hands and arms into the hitting area below my waist and on to impact, with my left hand guiding and my right hand ready to smash the ball. My swing is down and through the ball into the followthrough. My right arm straightens and my left arm folds into a natural, high followthrough. My driver contacts the ball slightly on the upswing.

I practise tee shots five balls at a time until I can cluster them close together on the range. I also practise fade and draw shots the same way. My average with the driver is 265 yards/242 metres.

Step 10: Sand

I use two types of shots from bunkers. The first is the pitch shot, which is easy to master. It is the same pitch shot practised under Step 4 Pitch Shots. My explosion shot is made with the sand wedge.

My stance is slightly open; heels are shoulder-width apart and dug into the sand. I play the ball 1 in/2.5 cm back from my left heel. I break my wrists quickly in the backswing; my grip pressure is firm. The clubface is slightly open and I hit 2 in/5 cm behind the ball. I follow through with the palm of my left hand downwards to keep the clubface open during the swing. I practise each shot five balls at a time until I can land them 1 ft/30 cm from the hole on the green.

Step 11: Playing Hilly Lies

- **Uphill:** Level the stance by bending your left knee and play the ball back in the stance. Using a lower-numbered club, swing slowly and smoothly, aiming to the right of the target.

- **Downhill:** Level the stance by bending your right knee. Play the ball back in the stance and use a more lofted club, swinging slowly and smoothly, aiming to the left of the target.

- **Sidehill – ball above your feet:** Keep the weight back on your heels. Play the ball from the middle of the stance. Grip the club on the end and aim to the left of the target.

- **Sidehill – ball below your feet:** Shorten the grip and, swinging slowly and smoothly, aim to the right of the target.

I practise all hilly lie shots five balls at a time, working until I land five near the pin.

Practising and Moving Up

As I worked up the staircase, my game continued to improve. When I finished work with the driver, I practised on the driving range, hitting five balls with every club, starting with the wedge, followed by the short irons, middle irons, long irons, fairway woods and, lastly, the driver. On the driving range, both the iron shots and the wood shots eventually became almost perfect. When my practice reached the long irons, I was already shooting scratch.

What a wonderful day when I had my first par round. I was playing the longer east course at Jacaranda. My partner that day was a 79-year-old gentleman, Joe, and he hit the ball straight for 150 yards/137 metres. Joe scored well with his straight, unerring shots. I had a habit of taking three practice swings with the driver, and on the second hole Joe asked me why. I told him I thought I needed them and he said, 'You swing like a pro. Have you ever noticed that the pros never take a practice swing?' I agreed to try just setting up, aiming and firing. I shot 72 that day, and Joe got a real kick out of my par since he had helped me to get it. I never again scored above par 72, as you can see from my collection of handicap cards – of which I am immensely proud!

GOLF HANDICAP CARD   HANDICAP
JOHN YOUNGBLOOD   7 *
PLANTATION GOLF CLUB
February 12, 1985   99578

MOST RECENT SCORES FIRST, LEFT TO RIGHT   LOW SCORE DIFFERENTIAL

74<	77<	78<	76<	74<	7.1
76<	79	83	78<	76<	AVERAGE
77<	75<	78	83	79	78.7 LAST 20 AVERAGE
80	78	79	85	89	

< INDICATES SCORES USED IN COMPUTATIONS   SCORES THIS CYCLE

GEO. LUMSDEN, P.G.A.   8

GOLF HANDICAP CARD   HANDICAP
JOHN YOUNGBLOOD   3
PLANTATION GOLF CLUB
Jun 11, 1986   98400

MOST RECENT SCORES FIRST, LEFT TO RIGHT   LOW SCORE DIFFERENTIAL

| 72 | 72< | 73 | 74 | 76 | 3.0 AVERAGE |

< INDICATES SCORES USED IN COMPUTATIONS   LAST 20 AVERAGE 73.4

BOBBY GOODMAN, P.G.A.   SCORES THIS CYCLE 5/86

GOLF HANDICAP CARD   HANDICAP
JOHN YOUNGBLOOD   2 *
PLANTATION GOLF CLUB
July 17, 1986   98400

MOST RECENT SCORES FIRST, LEFT TO RIGHT   LOW SCORE DIFFERENTIAL

72	72	71<	72	71	2.5 AVERAGE
72	72<	72<	73	74	73.4 LAST 20 AVERAGE
76					

< INDICATES SCORES USED IN COMPUTATIONS   SCORES THIS CYCLE

BOBBY GOODMAN, P.G.A.   6

GOLF HANDICAP CARD   HANDICAP
JOHN YOUNGBLOOD   2
PLANTATION GOLF CLUB
August 13, 1986   98400

MOST RECENT SCORES FIRST, LEFT TO RIGHT   LOW SCORE DIFFERENTIAL

70<	71<	72	72	71<	2.13 AVERAGE
72	72	72	71<	72	72.1 LAST 20 AVERAGE
71<	72	72<	72<	73	
74	76				

< INDICATES SCORES USED IN COMPUTATIONS   SCORES THIS CYCLE

BOBBY GOODMAN, P.G.A.   6

GOLF HANDICAP CARD					HANDICAP
JOHN YOUNGBLOOD					2
PLANTATION GOLF CLUB					
September 15, 1986					98400
MOST RECENT SCORES FIRST, LEFT TO RIGHT					LOW SCORE DIFFERENTIAL 2.0
72	71<	73	70<	72	
71<	70<	71<	72	72	AVERAGE
71<	72	72	72	71<	LAST 20 AVERAGE
72	71<	72	72<	72<	71.6
< INDICATES SCORES USED IN COMPUTATIONS					SCORES THIS CYCLE
BOBBY GOODMAN, P.G.A.					6

GOLF HANDICAP CARD					HANDICAP
JOHN YOUNGBLOOD					1*
PLANTATION GOLF CLUB					
October 20, 1986					98400
MOST RECENT SCORES FIRST, LEFT TO RIGHT					LOW SCORE DIFFERENTIAL 1.5
72	71<	70<	69<	71<	
72	72	71<	73	70<	AVERAGE
72	71<	70<	71<	72	LAST 20 AVERAGE
72	71<	72	72	72	71.3
< INDICATES SCORES USED IN COMPUTATIONS					SCORES THIS CYCLE
BOBBY GOODMAN, P.G.A.					8

GOLF HANDICAP CARD					HANDICAP
JOHN YOUNGBLOOD					1
PLANTATION GOLF CLUB					
November 18, 1986					98400
MOST RECENT SCORES FIRST, LEFT TO RIGHT					LOW SCORE DIFFERENTIAL 1.0
72	72	70<	70<	69<	
71	70<	72	71	70<	AVERAGE
69<	71	72	72	71<	LAST 20 AVERAGE
73	70<	72	71<	70<	70.9
< INDICATES SCORES USED IN COMPUTATIONS					SCORES THIS CYCLE
BOBBY GOODMAN, P.G.A.					7

GOLF HANDICAP CARD					HANDICAP
JOHN YOUNGBLOOD					1
PLANTATION GOLF CLUB					
December 16, 1986					98400
MOST RECENT SCORES FIRST, LEFT TO RIGHT					LOW SCORE DIFFERENTIAL 1.0
72	72	70<	70<	69<	
71	70<	72	71	70<	AVERAGE
69<	71	72	72	71<	LAST 20 AVERAGE
73	70<	72	71<	70<	70.9
< INDICATES SCORES USED IN COMPUTATIONS					SCORES THIS CYCLE
BOBBY GOODMAN, P.G.A.					11/86

GOLF HANDICAP CARD					HANDICAP
JOHN YOUNGBLOOD					+1*
PLANTATION GOLF CLUB					
January 13, 1987					98400
MOST RECENT SCORES FIRST, LEFT TO RIGHT					LOW SCORE DIFFERENTIAL +0.9
71	69<	73	72	70<	
71	72	72	70<	70<	AVERAGE
69<	71	70<	72	71<	LAST 20 AVERAGE
70<	69<	71<	72	72	70.9
< INDICATES SCORES USED IN COMPUTATIONS					SCORES THIS CYCLE
BOBBY GOODMAN, P.G.A.					6

GOLF HANDICAP CARD					HANDICAP
JOHN YOUNGBLOOD					+1
PLANTATION GOLF CLUB					
February 23, 1987					98400
MOST RECENT SCORES FIRST, LEFT TO RIGHT					LOW SCORE DIFFERENTIAL +0.6
70<	70<	70<	69<	72	
71	70<	69<	73	69<	AVERAGE
72	70<	71	71	69<	LAST 20 AVERAGE
73	72	70<	71	72	70.7
< INDICATES SCORES USED IN COMPUTATIONS					SCORES THIS CYCLE
BOBBY GOODMAN, P.G.A.					13

I have also kept the computer print-out from my handicap service, which listed my name as number one in the service. I have included this in the book to demonstrate to you the success of my method and to encourage you to look forward to seeing your name at the top of your handicap service list.

Rank	Diff	Handicap	Player's name	Rank	Diff	Handicap	Player's name
1	+0.60	+0.6	Youngblood, John	41	19.8	19.0	Guller, Carl
2	+0.30	+0.3	Hall, Thurman	42	20.10	19.3	Carey, Frank
3	6.33	6.1	Leslie, George	43	20.30	19.5	Lynch, Jack
4	7.5	7.2	Haglof, Russell	44	20.33	19.5	Scheckton, John
5	8.29	8.0	Pollinger, Geor	45	20.43	19.6	Mongato, Jack P.
6	8.70	8.4	Haglof, Susan	46	20.50	19.7	Bryan, James P.
7	9.67	9.3	Murphy, Bill	47	20.67	19.8	Palmacci, Bob
8	10.67	10.2	Trificano, Terr	48	21.00	20.2	McCray, Rodger
9	11.00	10.6	Williams, Geor	49	21.00	20.2	Laird, Jay
10	11.10	10.7	Brittle, Walt	50	21.50	20.6	Fossati, Jules
11	11.20	10.8	Bauman, Harry	51	21.80	20.9	Adas, David
12	12.00	11.5	Kalo, Duane	52	22.00	21.1	Suprenant, Don
13	12.00	11.5	Cucchiro, Tony	53	22.30	21.4	Vanse, Denny
14	12.40	11.9	McCray, J.N.	54	22.30	21.4	Casey, Jim
15	12.50	12.5	Argentine, Nick	55	22.40	21.5	Winfield, Roy
16	12.70	12.2	Perry, Ken	56	22.50	21.6	Lund, Art
17	13.70	13.2	Vangas, Chas	57	22.70	21.8	Wunsch, Adam
18	13.75	13.2	Duffek, Paul	58	23.00	22.1	Pesce, Joe
19	13.80	13.2	Normandy, Mike	59	23.00	22.1	De Santis, Joe
20	14.00	13.4	Lewly, Dick	60	23.17	22.2	Randall, Jeff
21	14.10	13.5	Leavitt, Steve	61	23.50	22.6	Haywood, Curt A.
22	14.60	14.0	Thompson, M.J.	62	23.80	22.8	May, Le Roy
23	14.70	14.1	Sain, Don	63	24.40	23.4	Fitzgerald, Cha
24	15.10	14.5	Twerdow, Arthur	64	24.60	23.6	Weissing, Louis
25	15.14	14.5	Stovall, Dale	65	25.00	24.0	Ostrander, J.W.
26	15.57	14.9	Fratone, Rich	66	25.00	24.0	Johnson, John
27	16.00	15.4	Singer, Jerry	67	25.00	24.0	Battaglia, Sal
28	17.00	16.3	Rau, David	68	25.30	24.3	Hagberg, Dick
29	17.33	16.6	Heaton, Don	69	25.50	24.5	Childers, Frank
30	17.40	16.7	Wilson, Delbert	70	25.70	24.7	Marnovich, Tho
31	17.80	17.1	Hunt, Wm.	71	26.50	25.4	Hammer, H.J.
32	17.87	17.2	Dickmeyer, Jame	72	27.00	25.9	Kepke, Jim
33	18.40	17.7	Randall, Randy	73	28.33	27.2	Sullivan, Rick
34	19.25	18.5	Lunsford, Roy	74	29.40	28.2	Hill, Whitey
35	19.30	18.5	White, John	75	31.00	29.8	Blanton, Ed
36	19.30	18.5	Ageloff, Al	76	37.90	36.4	Bacile, Joe
37	19.50	18.7	Johnson, Robert	77	39.33	37.8	Brown, Helen
38	19.50	18.7	Dindia, Paul	78	....	....	Lange, Ed
39	19.50	18.7	Battaglia, Ross	79	....	....	Cusmano, Anthony
40	19.67	18.9	Hermsen, Jim				

Serviced by: Computer Golf Service, 1700 S.W. 12th Avenue, Boca Raton, FL 33432
for Plantation Golf Club, 7050 W. Broward, Plantation, FL.

Communicating the Message

When my success was really beginning to work and I hit all the clubs on the driving range, a crowd would gather to watch me hit. Near my last practice session at Jacaranda, the starter, Jay, came excitedly through the crowd and said, 'John, I don't know what you did to your swing to hit shots like that. In all my days I have never seen any pro hit the ball better.' I began to get inquiries and telephone calls, and people began to ask me to write up the fundamentals and my practice procedure and give them a copy.

At the nineteenth hole one day, discussing how I dropped from a 28 handicap to scratch, several people asked why I didn't put my programme into a book. My nephew Robert also backed the idea. He was a fine teacher, and I respected his opinion very much. I had always felt that no-one would be interested in a book written by an ordinary golfer but, as my success continued, I began to think that, after all, my programme might be something special and I decided to begin to write it up. Little did I realise the problems I would experience in putting together a book on so technical a subject as golf, but I did have some experience of technical writing from my business background, so I accepted the challenge.

I had read that 90 per cent of golfers play between 90 and 100 strokes a round and that they are always seeking to better their handicaps. That must provide a market for a book – even one written by someone without professional training – if it offered them the chance to break out of the stalemate. Also, statistics prove that many people who would like to learn to play golf feel that it is too expensive, both in equipment and lessons to learn. My book would also be ideal for beginners.

Reams of paper and six months later, I had the first draft of what was to become *The Senior's Golf School*. I obviously wanted to find an expert golfer to demonstrate my principles and practice for the photographs, and I was lucky enough to find that Paul Azinger – then a young professional making a big impact on the circuit – was impressed by both my system and what I had achieved in using it, and he agreed to be involved in the project. Paul was happy to pose for the Ultimate Golf Swing Fundamentals that I developed, not his personal swing.

Now you have this book in your hands, you can put the principles into practice and achieve just the same dramatic improvement that I did. With assiduous practice on my system, your game will improve – and you'll find that it becomes much more enjoyable along the way.

By the way, the improvement doesn't have to stop at 72. I continued to play and practise and reached a scoring average of 70.6. The Ultimate Golf Swing Fundamentals and the Step-by-step Learning and Practice Programme helped me to accomplish all this. It worked for me – and it can work for you too!

CHAPTER 2
GOLF CLUBS AND EQUIPMENT

For those who are completely new to the game, the first thing to do is to learn a little about the equipment you need, and obviously the first and most vital thing is a set of golf clubs. Those who are already equipped and wanting to improve their game, can skip over this chapter.

A complete set of golf clubs is composed of 14 clubs – usually a selection of those listed on the right – each one specially designed to do a specific job. As in any skill, you will only get the best results if you use the right tool for the job, so learn about the clubs and their uses so that you can make the right selections when you are playing. Good decisions will make a real difference to your game and that, of course, will again increase your confidence.

There are various components to each club, and you should familiarise yourself with the correct terminology.

Iron clubs are made from forgings or castings of iron or stainless steel. Metal-wood clubs have now completely replaced wooden clubs, and graphite and titanium are now used in the club heads and shafts of woods. Because some golfers feel that they can hit more easily with woods, manufacturers now offer complete sets composed of woods. There is also a trend to make special clubs and set of clubs for seniors including, for instance, a 7 wood.

The Woods

- **Driver:** Used from the tee to the fairway.
- **7 wood:** Used from the rough and fairway. It is easier to hit than a long iron and good for seniors.
- **5 wood:** Used from the tee and for fairway shots.
- **4 wood:** Used from the tee and for fairway shots.
- **3 wood:** Used from the tee and for fairway shots.

The Irons

- **9 iron:** Used for short shots to the pin.
- **8 iron:** Used for short shots to the pin.
- **7 iron:** Used for shots from the fairway to the green.
- **6 iron:** Used for shots from the fairway to the green.
- **5 iron:** Used for shots from the fairway to the green.
- **4 iron:** Used for shots from the fairway to the green.
- **3 iron:** Used for shots from the fairway to the green.
- **2 iron:** Used for shots from the fairway to the green.
- **1 iron:** Used from the tee and for fairway shots.
- **Pitching wedge:** Used for accurate pitch shots.
- **Sand wedge:** Used for sand shots and pitch shots.
- **Lob wedge:** Used for green-side pitching.
- **Putter:** Used for putting on the green, from the fringe and from sand.

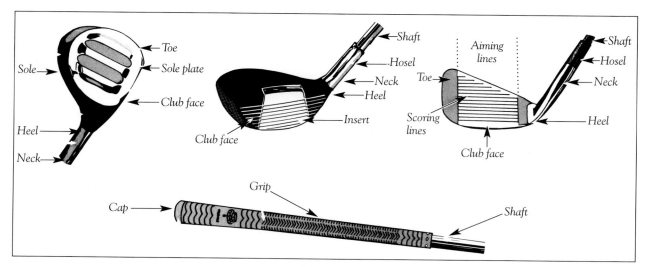

Golf club components.

Choosing your Equipment

The maximum number of clubs allowed by the rules of golf is 14. Golf clubs – as well as balls and all golf equipment – are manufactured to rigid specifications. A matched set of golf clubs are manufactured so that when the clubs are soled at the address position – the clubhead is placed on the ground ready to hit the ball – the cap ends of the shaft of each club will form a parallel line with the ground. This allows the same address position with each club, regardless of length. As the clubs grow shorter, the player's hands move closer to the body.

New players should have their clubs fitted by a PGA professional. Comfortable clubs are a must for good golf scores. It is a considerable outlay, so you want to get a suitable set. Such clubs will pay dividends in good scoring, and it is a pleasure to hit with clubs fitted to one's own frame.

Beginners can buy a 'short set', with fewer than 14 clubs. Matching clubs can be added later, as required.

Along with clubs, the player will need the following: a golf bag, shoes, golf glove, tees, balls and score cards.

Golf Club Average Specifications

Club	Lie	Loft	Length
Driver	55°	11°	43¼ in/110 cm
7 wood	56°	25°	42½ in/107 cm
5 wood	56°	22°	41¼ in/105 cm
4 wood	55¾°	19°	41¾ in/106 cm
3 wood	55½°	16°	42½ in/108 cm
9 iron	62°	46°	35½ in/90 cm
8 iron	61½°	42°	36 in/91 cm
7 iron	61°	38°	36½ in/93 cm
6 iron	60½°	34°	37 in/94 cm
5 iron	60°	30°	37½ in/95 cm
4 iron	58½°	26°	38 in/96 cm
3 iron	59°	23°	38½ in/98 cm
2 iron	58½°	20°	38½ in/98 cm
1 iron	58°	18°	39½ in/100 cm
Pitching wedge	63°	51°	35 in/89 cm
Lob wedge	63°	56°	35 in/89 cm
Sand iron	63°	57°	35 in/89 cm

3   Finish short pitch shots with the clubface facing up towards the sky. Keep the left wrist firm and facing the target at the finish.

4   Hit down on the ball and contact the ball first, then the turf.

5   Practise by lining up three balls in a row, 10 in/25 cm apart. Try to land each ball at the same spot.

6   Plan the shot to cover all levels of the green. Make sure the selected club and the swing will produce the shot to reach the target.

7   Keep the shoulders parallel to the target line when opening the stance.

8   Hit crisply through the ball. Do not swing 'at the ball', or slow down during the downswing.

9   Play the pitch-and-run shot with a 7 iron or 8 iron. The stroke produces a lower shot which will run on the green.

10 Use the short pitch and the pitch-and-run shots from the fairway, 50 yards/48 metres into the green.

11 Use a waist-high backswing to move the ball 40–50 yards/36–46 metres.

12 Use a one-third swing to move the ball 20–40 yards/18–36 metres.

13 Try short pitch and pitch-and-run shots from various distances from the green.

14 Swing the arms freely and smoothly for the short pitch shot. Develop rhythm by using a light grip pressure. Keep the same grip pressure throughout the stroke. Never hurry the shot. On this shot, the ball goes softly through the air and settles gently on the green.

Pitch Shots

Pitch shots are made from 50–100 yards/46–90 metres from the green. Pitch shots are made with the 6 iron, the 7 iron, the 8 iron and the 9 iron. The pitching wedge and the sand wedge can also be used. The motion in the pitch shots relates to the underhand motion in tossing a ball.

Pitch shots are high, lofting shots. The full backswing reaches just above the waist. The wrists hinge slightly and there is a slight degree of weight shift to the right foot. The followthrough is slightly longer than the backswing.

Pitch shots may be hit by gripping down on the shaft 1–2 in/2.5–5 cm from the butt of the shaft to provide steadier control of the club.

The Address for the Pitch Shot

1   Assume the open stance. Heels should be 10 in/25 cm apart.

2   Keep the knees slightly flexed.

3   The weight should be slightly on the left foot.

4   Place the hands ahead of the ball.

5   Keep the eyes over the ball.

6   Keep the ball ahead of the right heel, towards the centre of the stance.

7   Bend forwards from the hips until the arms hang free.

8   Play the ball fairly close to the feet. Swing back slowly, keeping the right elbow close to the body.

The Swing for the Pitch Shot

The swing moves the triangle of the shoulders, arms and hands as a pendulum, back until the wrists start to cock. There is a slight shift of the weight to the right foot in the full backswing, which reaches just past the hips. The triangle is swung down on the same path, returning to the address position at impact and then through the ball into the followthrough. The weight transfers to the left leg on the downswing. The hands stay ahead of the clubhead through impact.

Body movements are minimised in the pitch shot. Aim pitch shots to land on the green, near the pin. Practise pitch shots from varying distances from 50–100 yards/46–90 metres from the green.

Suggestions for Better Pitch Shots

1 Swing with light grip pressure.

2 Swing back to just above the waist to allow the weight to transfer to the right foot.

3 Use a descending stroke.

4 Be careful in opening the stance and keep the shoulders parallel to the target line.

5 Swing through the ball. Don't swing 'at the ball'.

6 Let the clubhead lift the ball. Do not 'scoop' or lift the hands.

7 Count 'one and two' when swinging to improve timing and rhythm.

8 Hit crisply and firmly, and follow through.

9 Control the length of the shot by the length of the backswing and the followthrough.

10 Control balance throughout the full swing. This is a must in all golf shots.

11 Use the pitch-and-run shot if the green is hard and dry, because a pitch shot won't bite.

12 Close the clubface slightly to cause the ball to roll more on the green when playing the pitch-and-run shot from the 100 ft/30 metre area.

13 Aim pitch shots at the top of the flagstick. This prevents shots that are short of the green.

14 Play the high fade pitch shot with the shoulders, hips and feet aligned slightly to the left of the target line. Make sure the club faces the target. Play the ball opposite the left heel. Do not let the right hand cross the left during or just after impact. Use this slightly cut shot to produce a floating fade, dropping on the green.

Playing from Hilly Lies

- **Uphill:** Level the stance by bending the left knee. Use a lower-numbered club and play the ball back in the stance. Aim to the right of the target. Lean slightly forwards to maintain balance. Swing slow and smooth.

- **Downhill:** Level the stance by bending the right knee. Use the open stance. Use a more lofted club. Play the ball back in the stance. Aim to the left of the target. Swing slow and smooth.

- **Sidehill (ball below feet):** Keep the weight back on the heels. Grip the club on the end. Play the ball from the middle of the stance. Aim to the left of the target.

- **Sidehill (ball above feet):** Shorten the grip and shorten the swing. Swing slow and smooth. Aim to the right of the target.

Stance for Pitch Shots from the Fairway

1   Assume an open stance. Heels are 10 in/25 cm apart.

2   Flex the knees slightly.

3   Weight should be slightly on the target foot.

4   Place the hands ahead of the ball.

5   Keep the eyes over the ball.

6   Place the ball ahead of the right heel, towards the centre of the stance.

7   Bend forwards from the hips.

One-quarter Backswing for Pitch Shots from the Fairway

1   The swing moves the triangle of the shoulders, arms and hands as a pendulum.

2   Swing back one-quarter and keep the triangle in a straight line with the club.

One-half Backswing (full) for Pitch Shots from the Fairway

1 The swing moves the triangle back until the wrists start to cock.

2 The full backswing reaches just past hip height.

One-quarter Downswing for Pitch Shots from the Fairway

1 The swing is made around a steady spine.

2 Keep the right knee in the same position and flex throughout the swing.

Impact for Pitch Shots from the Fairway

1 Transfer the weight to the left leg in the downswing.

2 Keep the hands ahead of the clubhead through impact.

One-half Followthrough for Pitch Shots from the Fairway

1 Minimise body movements in the pitch shot.

2 Aim pitch shots to land on the green, near the pin.

Three-quarter (full) Followthrough for Pitch Shots from the Fairway

1 Swing with a light grip pressure.

2 Swing through the ball. Don't swing 'at the ball'.

3 Let the clubhead lift the ball. Don't 'scoop' or lift the hands.

Stance for Downhill Pitch Shots from the Fairway

1 Bend the right knee to attain a level stance.

Stance for Uphill Pitch Shots from the Fairway

1 Assume an open stance. Feet are 10 in/25 cm apart.

2 Place the ball near the target heel.

3 Hold the head behind the ball.

The Short Irons

The short irons and the average distances to the pin are:

- **Sand wedge**   75 yards/68 metres.
- **Pitching wedge** 105 yards/96 metres.
- **9 iron**   115 yards/105 metres.
- **8 iron**   125 yards/114 metres.
- **7 iron**   135 yards/123 metres.

Short irons can be used for pitch shots, shots from the rough, high grass and fairway bunkers. A full swing, with the backswing to shoulder-height for the hands, is required to attain the distances listed above. The full swing for a short iron shot is a three-quarter swing, which is recommended for all iron shots in the learning period for beginning players.

When practising short iron shots, start with the pitching wedge and hit shots to a green 50 yards/46 metres away. Practise at a practice green or a driving range. Hit shots until you can land ten in a row on the green and continue until five shots out of ten land within 10 feet/3 metres of the pin.

When you have reached proficiency with the wedge shots, set up practice sessions with the 9 iron, the 8 iron and the 7 iron. Hit these shots directly over the same green used with the wedge, to the full distance with each iron. Accurate approach shots with the short irons are vital to low scoring in the game of golf.

The Address for Short Iron Shots

1 Assume an open stance. Keep the feet 10 in/ 25 cm apart.

2 Turn the toe-cap one-quarter turn to the left.

3 Play the ball from the centre between the feet.

4   Keep the hips and shoulders square with the target line when moving the left foot back in opening the stance.

5   Favour the weight on the target foot.

6   Keep the hands well ahead of the ball.

7   Flex the knees.

8   Bend forwards from hips.

9   Grip the club firmly for short iron shots.

10 Relax and make sure the stance is comfortable.

The Swing with the Short Irons

When beginning the backswing, make certain that you take a level turn around the spine, without swaying, dipping or changing the angle of the back, shoulders or hips. Keep the head steady and move the triangle straight back from the ball past the rear foot. Keeping the left arm straight, turn the triangle around the spine to a full backswing just shoulder high. The wrists will cock naturally and the back will face the target. The hips will turn less than the shoulders. The club will point over the right shoulder towards the target.

The downswing begins by turning the left hip to the left, which pulls the hands down. The right elbow is close to the right hip and the hands continue down into the hitting area below the waist. The weight begins on the left foot and stays there throughout the shot. The head stays behind the ball and at impact the right hand hits down and through the ball, with the left hand guiding the club. The hit is made with the hands leading the clubhead and the swing continues to a high followthrough.

Stance for Short Iron Shots from the Fairway

1   Assume an open stance. Feet are 10 in/25 cm apart. Target foot is turned left one-quarter.

2   Play the ball centred between the feet.

3   Weight should slightly favour the target foot.

4   Hold the hands ahead of the ball.

5   Flex the knees.

6   Bend forwards from the hips.

One-quarter Backswing for Short Iron Shots from the Fairway

1 Make a level turn around the spine, without swaying or dipping or changing the angle of the back, shoulders and hips.

One-half Backswing for Short Iron Shots from the Fairway

1 Keep the head steady and move the triangle straight back from the ball past the right foot.

2 Keep the left arm straight and turn the triangle back one-half as shown.

Three-quarter (full) Backswing for Short Iron Shots from the Fairway

One-half Downswing for Short Iron Shots from the Fairway

1   A full backswing is just shoulder high.

2   The wrists cock naturally.

3   The back will face the target.

4   Turn the hips less than the shoulders are turned.

5   Point the club over the right shoulder towards the target.

1   Begin the downswing by turning the left hip to the left, which pulls the hands down.

2   Keep the right elbow close to the right hip.

3   Be sure the head is behind the ball.

Three-quarter Downswing for Short Iron Shots from the Fairway

1   The weight is on the left foot and stays there throughout the shot.

2   Make sure the hands are entering the hitting area below the waist.

Impact for Short Iron Shots from the Fairway

1   The right hand hits down and through the ball, with the left hand guiding the club.

2   Hit with the hands leading the clubhead.

One-half Followthrough for Short Iron Shots from the Fairway

1 Don't quit on short iron shots. Hit down, contacting the ball first, then taking turf by hitting through the ball.

2 Keep the left arm fully extended until the ball is well on its way, for accuracy on short iron shots.

Three-quarter Followthrough for Short Iron Shots from the Fairway

1 Hit with the hands leading the clubhead.

2 The swing continues to a high followthrough in perfect balance.

Full Followthrough for Short Iron Shots from the Fairway

1 The swing continues through impact and out towards the target.

2 The right arm straightens and the left arm folds into a high followthrough.

Suggestions for Better Short Iron Shots

1 Hit down, contacting the ball first, then take turf by hitting through the ball. Don't quit on short iron shots.

2 Do not 'swing at', or try to 'scoop' the ball.

3 Do not stand too far from the ball so that reaching for the ball is necessary. Also, do not stand too close.

4 Choke (grip down) the club shaft 1–2 in/2.5–5 cm if the shot feels more comfortable.

5 Make certain that the clubface covers the ball on the backswing.

6 Keep the left arm fully extended until the ball is well on its way, for accuracy in short iron shots. Also, keep the wrists firm.

7 Hit a fade by playing the ball up near the left heel with the weight slightly on the left foot. Be sure that the right hand does not turn over after impact.

8 Keep the weight on the target foot throughout the swing for a low shot. Play the ball back past the centre of the stance. Swing the clubhead downwards into the turf after impact.

9 Use a lower-numbered club for longer shots.

The Middle Irons

The middle irons and the average distances with these clubs are:

- **6 iron** — 145 yards/133 metres.
- **5 iron** — 155 yards/142 metres.
- **4 iron** — 165 yards/151 metres.

The middle irons are used for full shots from the fairway to the green. They are also used for long bunker shots. When hitting the green with a middle iron, stay with the shot through the followthrough. Don't quit on the shot or look up too soon. The swing with the middle iron is compact, the grip firm and the backswing short. The stance is more upright, as the length of the club dictates.

The Address for the Middle Irons

1. Assume an open stance. Keep the feet 14 in/ 36 cm apart.

2. Place the weight on the target foot.

3. Position the hands ahead of the ball.

4. Play the ball back towards the centre of the stance.

5. Take the proper grip.

6. Flex the knees.

7. Bend forwards from the hips.

8. Relax and keep the head still.

The Swing with the Middle Irons

With the left arm straight and dominant and the right arm soft, move the triangle of the shoulders, arms and hands straight back from the ball past the right foot and continue upwards to a three-quarter backswing. The shoulders will turn fully with the back to the target and the hips will turn less. The club will point over the right shoulder towards the target. There will be some natural cocking of the wrists. Swing the club smoothly to the top of the backswing, counting 'one and two' or 'back and through'. Counting should be used in all shots, including putts.

The downswing begins by turning the hips to the left, causing the weight to begin transferring to the target leg. This drops the triangle towards the waist and on towards the right knee and right foot as the hands and arms move into the hitting area. The body stays steady and the triangle swings into the impact area, with the left arm guiding and the right hand read to smash the ball. The body position at impact is about the same as at the address.

The swing continues through impact and on towards the target, the right arm straightening and the left arm folding into a natural followthrough. The swing will have been done around the spine. The address posture stays the same throughout the swing. As the triangle moves down towards the waist in the downswing, the right shoulder moves down and under while the hands move towards impact and the followthrough.

Stance for Middle Iron Shots from the Fairway

1 Assume an open stance. Feet are 14 in/36 cm apart.

2 Weight should be on the target foot.

3 Play the ball towards the centre of the stance.

4 Keep the hands ahead of the ball.

5 Flex the knees.

6 Bend forwards from the hips.

7 Relax and keep the head still.

One-quarter Backswing for Middle Iron Shots from the Fairway

1 Turn around the spine and move the triangle to the one-quarter backswing position.

2 Keep the left arm straight.

One-half Backswing for Middle Iron Shots from the Fairway

1 The swing continues upwards until the club is parallel with the ground.

2 Point the left knee behind the ball.

Three-quarter (full) Backswing for Middle Iron Shots from the Fairway

1 Turn the shoulders fully with the back to the target, and the hips will turn less.

2 Point the club over the right shoulder towards the target.

One-half Downswing for Middle Iron Shots from the Fairway

1 Begin the downswing by turning the hips to the left, causing the weight to transfer to the target leg.

2 This drops the triangle towards the waist.

Three-quarter Downswing for Middle Iron Shots from the Fairway

1 Keep the body steady as the arms and hands move into the hitting area, with the right hand ready to smash the ball.

Impact for Middle Iron Shots from the Fairway

1 Keep the body position at impact about the same as at the address.

One-half Followthrough for Middle Iron Shots from the Fairway

1 The swing continues through impact on out towards the target.

2 The right arm straightens in the one-half followthrough.

Three-quarter Followthrough for Middle Iron Shots from the Fairway

1 Fold the left arm into a natural followthrough.

2 The swing is around the spine.

Full Followthrough for Middle Iron Shots from the Fairway

1 Face the target with the body in a natural, comfortable followthrough.

Suggestions for Better Middle Iron Shots

1 Perfect the middle iron clubs by determining the distance you can hit with each club. Hit with a smooth and easy swing.

2 Practise by hitting five balls at a time until you can hit them the same distance and to the same spot. Do this with each club. Record your distance.

3 Be sure the club you select will clear the lip when hitting from fairway bunkers.

4 Hit middle irons so that the clubface contacts the ball first, before contacting the turf. The shot will fail if this is not accomplished correctly.

5 Be certain that the hands lead the clubhead when swinging middle irons through impact.

6 Stand the right distance from the ball. Do not reach or stand too close.

7 Grip the club firmly and make the backswing slightly steeper and more upright when hitting from heavy grass. Make the downswing firm and sharp. Try to contact the ball before the heavy grass.

8 Hit only straight shots until you complete the beginner's instruction section. Curving shots will be covered in the advanced instruction section.

The Long Irons

The long irons and their average distances are:
- **3 iron**   175 yards/160 metres.
- **2 iron**   185 yards/169 metres.

The long irons are used in long shots from the fairway. When hitting for the green, make certain that the longer backswing and the forward swing are rhythmic and smooth. The swing with the long irons is more sweeping, similar to sweeping shots with the fairway woods from a good lie. But, if the lie is tight, the stroke must be downwards, striking the ball first and then the turf. In the backswing, the hands should reach no higher than the back of the shoulder.

The Address for the Long Iron Shot

1 Assume a square stance. Keep the feet 18 in/46 cm apart.

2 Place the weight slightly on the left foot.

3 Position the hands slightly ahead of the ball.

4 Place the ball 4 in/10 cm back from the left heel.

5 Flex the knees.

6 Bend forwards from the hips, not the waist.

7 Relax and keep the head still.

8 Keep the body comfortably erect.

The Swing with the Long Iron

With the left arm straight and the right arm soft, move the triangle of the shoulders, arms and hands back from the ball past the rear foot, then continue upwards to a full backswing, with the wrists cocked just above shoulder level. The shoulders will turn fully, so the player's back is to the target. The hips will turn less. The club will point over the right shoulder towards the target.

The downswing begins by turning the hips to the left, which causes the weight to begin transferring to the left leg, which also drops the triangle towards the waist and towards the right knee and right foot as the hands and arms move into the hitting area. The body stays steady and the triangle swings into the impact area, with the left arm guiding and the right hand ready to smash the ball. The swing is down and through the ball. The ball is struck first and turf taken after, but not as much turf is taken as for the middle irons. The body position at impact is about the same as it was at the address.

The swing continues through impact and on towards the target, the right arm straightening and the left arm folding into a natural followthrough facing the target. The swing has been around the spine. The posture at the address stays the same throughout the swing. As the triangle moves downwards, towards the waist in the downswing, the right shoulder moves down and under, as the triangle moves towards impact and followthrough.

Difficult Plays with the Long Irons

- **Playing from the Rough:** Grip the club firmly. Make the backswing slightly steeper and make the downswing firm and sharp. Try to contact the ball before the rough. Keep the head steady.

- **Playing into the Wind:** Use two clubs longer than usual. Keep the ball low. Estimate the effect of the wind on the shot.

- **Playing with the Wind:** Keep the body steady. Do not sway or hurry the shot. Hit firmly and solidly – the ball will lose some spin and roll more than normal.

- **Cross Winds:** Estimate the effect of the wind on the shot. Correct the shot to have the wind bring the ball back into the intended target line.

- **Playing from Sand:** Use the pitch shot swing. Open the stance with the feet worked into the sand. Hit 3 in/7.5 cm behind the ball. Swing low and smooth and into a full followthrough.

Stance for Long Iron Shots from the Fairway

1 Assume a square stance. Feet are 18 in/46 cm apart.

2 Keep the hands slightly ahead of the ball.

3 Place the ball 4 in/10 cm back from target heel.

4 Flex the knees.

5 Bend forwards from the hips.

6 Keep the body comfortably erect.

One-quarter Backswing for Long Iron Shots from the Fairway

1 Straighten the left arm, keep the right arm soft and move the triangle back to the one-quarter backswing position.

One-half Backswing for Long Iron Shots from the Fairway

1 The body turns around a steady spine.

2 The swing moves upwards to the one-half position.

Three-quarter Backswing (full) for Long Iron Shots from the Fairway

1 The swing continues to a full backswing, the wrists cocked just above shoulder level.

2 Point the club over the right shoulder towards the target.

One-half Downswing for Long Iron Shots from the Fairway

1 Begin the downswing by turning the hips to the left. This causes the weight to transfer to the target foot, and the hands and arms move downwards.

Three-quarter Downswing for Long Iron Shots from the Fairway

1 Move the hands and arms into the hitting area.

2 The left arm guides and the right hand is ready to smash the ball.

Impact for Long Iron Shots from the Fairway

1 The swing continues through impact on and out towards the target.

2 Contact the ball first, turf taken after, but take less than for middle iron shots.

One-half Followthrough for Long Iron Shots from the Fairway

1 As the triangle moves downwards in the downswing, and as the right shoulder moves down and under, the triangle moves towards impact and the followthrough.

Three-quarter Followthrough for Long Iron Shots from the Fairway

1 The swing has been made around the spine, as the posture at the address stays the same throughout the swing.

Full Followthrough for Long Iron Shots from the Fairway

1 The swing continues through impact on out towards the target, into a natural and comfortable followthrough.

Suggestions for Better Long Iron Shots

1 Take a full shoulder turn on the backswing.

2 Let the club do the work; don't force the shot. Hit smoothly and with good timing.

3 Let the loft and the length of the clubshaft take care of distance. Trust the club to do this.

4 Be certain that the clubhead is swinging down at impact, so that turf is taken in front of the ball after you hit the ball.

5 Let the one-piece swing move the shoulders, arms, hands and hips all at the same time on the backswing and the downswing.

6 Make the stance comfortable at the address and keep the head and body in the same relative position throughout the swing.

7 Play the ball 4 in/10 cm back from the left heel when hitting from a good lie. Take a smooth swing and aim at the green.

8 Play the ball further back, from a cupped lie and swing firmly down through impact.

9 Keep the arms close at the address. Keep the right elbow close to the right hip in the backswing. Keep the arms close together in the downswing and followthrough.

10 Swing the long irons with the same force as the middle irons. They do not require a harder swing.

11 Work on long iron shots by aiming shots to land at the same spot.

12 Concentrate on these swing reminders: 'back and through', 'back and shift', 'stretch and swing', 'one and two', 'one and two, wait three', 'back and smooth'.

The Fairway Woods

The fairway woods and their distances are as follows:
- **5 wood**   185 yards/169 metres.
- **4 wood**   200 yards/183 metres.
- **3 wood**   225 yards/206 metres.

Fairway woods can be used for tee shots and good lies in the fairway and good lies in the rough. They may be hit from fairway bunkers if the ball is sitting up and the lip is not too high for the shot to clear. The ball should be picked clean from the sand.

When hitting a 3 wood from the fairway from a good lie, hit with a sweeping stroke and do not take turf. The swing is much like the swing you will learn to use with the driver.

Tight lies should be hit slightly on the downswing, nipping the ball first, and taking a little turf. Lies in the rough must be hit firmly downwards. The 4 wood can be used from any lie, using the sweeping stroke for good lies and hitting downwards on all others. The 4 wood can also be hit from the tee.

The 5 wood can be hit from the tee, and for shorter distances from the fairway. The 5 wood can be hit from all lies, using the sweeping stroke for good lies and the downward stroke for tight lies. The 5 wood is a good club from the rough if hit from reasonably good lies.

The Address for the Fairway Woods

1   Assume a square stance. Keep heels 20 in/51 cm apart.

2   Weight should be slightly on the left foot.

3   Place the ball 2 in/5 cm back from the left heel.

4   Keep the hands slightly ahead of the ball.

5   Keep the body square to the target line, and comfortably erect.

6   Flex the knees.

7   Bend from the hips.

8   Take the proper grip.

The Swing with the Fairway Woods

The swing with the fairway wood begins with the left arm straight and the right arm soft. Move the triangle of the shoulders, arms and hands straight back from the ball and past the right foot and continue upwards to a full backswing.

The wrists will cock naturally, no higher than the top of the head. The shoulders will turn fully with the back facing the target. The hips will turn less than the shoulders. The club will point over the right shoulder towards the target.

The downswing begins by turning the hips to the left, causing the weight to transfer to the target leg. This drops the triangle towards the waist and the rear foot as the arms and hands move into the hitting area.

The body stays steady and the triangle swings into the impact area with the left arm guiding and the right hand ready to smash the ball. The swing is down and through the ball. The ball is struck first and a little turf is taken after contact. A ball sitting up in a good lie will need a sweeping stroke that does not take turf. The downward stroke is to be used for tight lies. The body position at impact is about the same as at the address.

As the swing continues through impact and on towards the target, the right arm straightens and the left arm folds into a naturally high followthrough. The swing has been around the spine. The address posture stays the same throughout the swing. As the triangle moves downwards in the downswing, the right shoulder moves down and under as the triangle moves towards impact and the followthrough.

Stance for Fairway Wood Shots

1 Assume a square stance. Feet are 20 in/51 cm apart.

2 Weight should be slightly on the target foot.

3 Place the ball 2 in/5 cm back from the target heel.

4 Keep the hands slightly ahead of the ball.

5 Keep the body erect and square to the target line.

6 Flex the knees.

7 Bend from the hips.

8 Take the proper grip.

One-quarter Backswing for Fairway Wood Shots

1 Begin the swing with the left arm straight and the right arm soft.

2 The triangle moves the club straight back from the ball to the one-quarter position.

One-half Backswing for Fairway Wood Shots

1   The swing continues upwards to the one-half position.

2   Turn the body around a steady spine.

Full Backswing for Fairway Wood Shots

1   Use a three-quarter backswing for fairway wood shots.

2   Point the club over the right shoulder towards the target.

One-half Downswing for Fairway Wood Shots

1 Begin the downswing by turning the hips to the left. This causes the weight to transfer to the target leg. This drops the triangle towards the waist.

Three-quarter Downswing for Fairway Wood Shots

1 The swing continues down.

2 The arms and hands move into the hitting area.

Impact for Fairway Wood Shots

1 The swing is down and through the ball.

2 Contact the ball first, so a little turf is taken after.

3 Keep the body position at impact about the same as at the address.

One-half Followthrough for Fairway Wood Shots

1 The swing through impact continues on out towards the target.

2 Hold the head still in the starting position.

Three-quarter Followthrough for Fairway Wood Shots

1 Straighten the right arm as the left arm is folding.

2 Move the right shoulder down and under.

Full Followthrough for Fairway Wood Shots

1 Notice that this is a natural, high followthrough.

2 You should swing around a steady spine.

Suggestions for Better Fairway Wood Shots

1 Practise fairway wood shots from a driving range or a practice fairway. Work on hitting from good lies and tight lies. Try to land all your shots close together.

2 Remember that the objective of the fairway wood shot is to place it in position for an easy iron shot to the green. A loss of backspin in fairway wood shots makes it hard to hold the ball on the green, but you should try to land the ball on the green anyway.

3 Swing fairway woods in a relaxed way. Trust the club to move the ball and never try for anything extra.

4 Keep the wrists high and straight at the address and keep them straight throughout the swing. Keep the body posture steady, with no tilting or dipping during the backswing, downswing and followthrough; to do otherwise spells disaster and your shot will not make the distance and direction you want.

5 Realise that the proper path of the clubhead in the hitting area moves the club from inside the target line, along the target line and back inside the target line. The clubhead should never pass outside the line. If this happens, the clubhead will cross the ball, causing an off-line shot.

6 Remember that the basic fundamentals of the golf swing are the same for every shot in golf. The swings are affected only by the length of the club.

7 Let the clubhead contact the ball and then the turf when hitting fairway woods off hard, dry areas of the fairway with little grass. Squeeze the ball off the turf. The swing is downwards, taking a little turf after contacting the ball.

8 Use fairway wood clubs for the shots on tight driving holes.

9 Grip down 1 in/2.5 cm on the clubshaft to hit soft 4 and 5 wood shots to the green.

10 Hit the driver from the fairway, if the lie is perfect, by gripping down $1\frac{1}{2}$ in/4 cm on the clubshaft. The swing is the same as for a 3 wood swing.

The Driver: Tee Shots

The driver is the club that will produce the longest shot from the tee. The driver should be placed in position for the best angle for a shot to the green with a fairway wood or an iron. Tight, narrow fairways require finesse shots from the tee with the 3 or the 4 wood, depending on the distance needed. The greatest concern in tee shots is to keep the ball on the fairway and, on par 3 holes, to hit the green from the tee, though you very rarely require a driver on a par 3.

When standing on the tee, look down the fairway and visualise the best spot to land your drive. Notice any contours that could affect the shot and whether it would be better to place the ball to the left or to the right on the fairway. Keep a mental image of the spot where you want to land the ball as you set up for the shot and try to retain this image as you execute the swing.

The driver is the easiest club with which to hit. The swing must be co-ordinated, smooth and in balance, with the proper tempo. The ball cannot move from the tee until the player strokes it with his or her club.

The Address for the Drive

1 Let balance and relaxation start with the set-up for the next shot; they are important in the drive.

2 Assume a stance that is slightly closed, with the feet shoulder-width apart, or use a square or a slightly open stance.

3 The weight should be slightly on the right foot.

4 Place the ball 1 in/2.5 cm back from the left heel.

5 Keep the hands slightly behind the ball.

6 Flex the knees.

7 Keep the body square to the target line and comfortably erect.

8 Bend from the hips.

9 Take the proper grip.

10 Tap the heels. The legs should feel alive.

The Swing with the Driver

With the left arm straight and the right arm soft, move the triangle of the shoulders, arms and hands straight back from the ball past the right foot and continue upwards to a full backswing, with the wrists cocked naturally above the top of the head. The shoulders will turn fully until the back faces the target but the club will not be allowed to become horizontal at this stage of swing development.

The downswing begins by turning the left hip to the left, causing the weight to transfer to the target leg. This also drops the triangle towards the waist and the right foot, as the arms and hands move into the hitting area below the waist. The left arm will be guiding and the right arm and hand will be ready to smash the ball.

The swing is down and through the ball. The clubhead contacts the ball slightly on the upswing, sweeping the ball off the tee. The body stays steady throughout the swing. The body position at impact is approximately the same as it was at the address.

The swing continues through impact and towards the target, the right arm straightening and the left arm folding into a natural, high followthrough. The swing is around the spine. The address posture stays the same throughout the swing. As the triangle moves downwards in the downswing, the right shoulder moves down and under as the triangle moves towards impact and the followthrough.

Stance for Tee Shots with the Driver

1 Assume a slightly closed stance. The feet are shoulder-width apart.

2 Lean the weight slightly on the right foot.

3 Place the ball 1 in/2.5 cm back from the target heel.

4 Keep the hands slightly behind the ball.

5 Square the body to the target line and stay comfortably erect.

6 Bend from the hips.

7 Take the proper grip.

8 Tap the heels; the legs should feel alive.

9 Maintain balance and relaxation; they are important in the drive.

One-quarter Backswing with the Driver

1 The triangle moves the club straight back from the ball to the one-quarter position.

2 The left arm is straight and the right arm soft.

One-half Backswing with the Driver

1 Turn the body around the spine to move the triangle to the one-half backswing position.

Full Backswing with the Driver

1 The swing continues upwards to a full backswing, with the wrists cocked naturally above the top of the head.

2 Turn the shoulders full with the back facing the target. The hips turn less.

One-half Downswing with the Driver

1 Begin the downswing by turning the left hip to the left. This causes the weight to start transferring to the target leg.

2 Notice that this also drops the triangle to the waist.

Three-quarter Downswing with the Driver

1 Move the arms and hands into the hitting area below the waist.

Impact with the Driver

One-half Followthrough with the Driver

1 Guide the left arm as the right arm and hand smash the ball at impact.

2 Swing down and through the ball, sweeping the ball off the tee.

1 Contact the ball slightly on the upswing with the clubhead as it continues to the one-half followthrough position.

Three-quarter Followthrough with the Driver

1   Move the right shoulder down and under as the triangle moves into the three-quarter followthrough position.

Full Followthrough with the Driver

1   Notice that the swing has been around the spine.

2   Maintain a steady body throughout the swing.

Suggestions for Better Tee Shots

1 Tee the ball high, with about half the ball showing above the top of the clubhead when it is poised behind the ball.

2 Check the grip. The back of the left hand should face the target. The palm of the right hand interfaces with the left palm and also faces the target. Maintain an even grip pressure throughout all golf swings. Be firm with the last three fingers of the left hand. This will prevent loosening of the grip at the top of the backswing. The firm grip in the right hand should be in the two middle fingers.

3 Practise the wood clubs until you have attained consistency with form and results. Find a good form and repeat it until it is ingrained.

4 Do not stand too close or too far from the ball. If you do, it will throw your swing off balance.

5 Check the position of the feet; this is important. The left foot is turned one-quarter towards the target and the right foot is turned one-eighth to the right. Many players leave the right foot straight, but this is optional.

6 Keep the right elbow close to the body during the swing. This delays unhinging the wrists until the club has reached the hitting area, resulting in greater clubhead speed and longer distance.

7 Do not ground the clubhead at the address. Keep the club 1 in/2.5 cm off the ground to prevent stubbing on the take-away. This will help set the proper grip pressure and make for a smoother take-away.

8 Prevent swaying by never shifting the weight towards the outside of the feet. The weight should shift to the instep of the right foot during the backswing and on to (not outside) the left foot in the downswing.

9 Counteract centrifugal force in the downswing by addressing the shot with more weight towards the heels. Maintain the weight there throughout the backswing and downswing.

10 Face the back of the left hand down the target line as you strike the ball. At the address, think of backhanding the club face squarely into the back of the ball. This will result in longer, straighter shots.

11 Increase distance with good timing.

12 Follow this action sequence of the downswing. The left heel lowers and the hips turn to the left, transferring the weight to the left leg; the shoulders turn; the hands and arms start down; the clubhead moves down past the waist into the hitting area; then through impact and the followthrough.

Suggested Method for Using the Beginner's Instruction Section

1   Learn to putt.

2   Learn to chip with the 5 iron, the 7 iron and the 9 iron.

3   Learn to hit short pitch shots with the 7 iron, the 8 iron and the 9 iron.

4   Learn to hit pitch shots with the pitching wedge, the 9 iron, the 8 iron and the 7 iron.

5   Learn to hit the short irons: the 7 iron, the 8 iron, the 9 iron, the pitching wedge and the sand wedge.

6   Learn to hit the middle irons: the 4 iron, the 5 iron and the 6 iron.

7   Learn to hit the long irons: the 2 iron and the 3 iron.

8   Learn to hit the fairway woods: the 3 wood, the 4 wood and the 5 wood.

9   Learn to hit tee shots with the driver, the 3 wood, the 4 wood and the 5 wood.

Diligent use of this programme in sequence should produce a sound swing. Practice and playing should produce the skill to break 80 on a par 72 golf course. When you have broken 80, proceed to the advanced golf instruction section (see chapter 5) and work for further progress to any goal you desire to set for your achievement.

Suggested Practice Procedure

At each session, try to practise as follows:

1   Putting.

2   Chipping.

3   Short pitch and pitch-and-run shots.

4   Short iron shots.

5   Middle iron shots.

6   Long iron shots.

7   Fairway wood shots.

8   Tee shots.

CHAPTER 5
THE ULTIMATE GOLF SWING FUNDAMENTALS

This chapter covers the detailed step-by-step programme for improving your golf swing. Before we start, however, it is important to understand some basic golfing concepts, which will help you put the fundamentals into practice.

Golf Concepts

Arc
The arc of the swing is the invisible path made in the air by swinging the clubhead. The arc is described by the clubhead and the length of the club. There will be long arcs and shorter arcs, depending on the length of the club.

The long arc is used with the woods and the long irons. The medium arc is used with the middle irons. The short arc is used with the short irons.

To determine the low point of the arc with an iron, take practice swings until a divot is taken. Practise until the turf is taken at the proper spot with the iron you are swinging. This will be the low point of the arc with that iron.

Plane
The air space within the arc of your swing around the spine is the plane of the swing. As the swing moves into the backswing, the plane will be upright, flat or in between these two planes. The plane will be determined by the player's height and build.

Set up in a comfortable position, relaxed and balanced. Swing back and accelerate through the ball.

The inside-out plane starts inside the target line, moves along it and then moves inside in the followthrough. This plane is used with the middle irons.

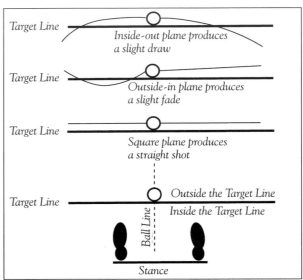

The three basic planes.

The outside-in plane starts at the target line, then drifts out and stays outside at impact. This plane I used with short iron shots.

The square plane begins along the target line, moves inside the line and returns square to the ball to a full followthrough. This plane should be used with the long irons and the woods.

The swing has three dimensions: backwards, upwards and around. These correspond to the backswing, downswing and the followthrough.

Full shots will have length, trajectory, direction and curve. The clubhead face must be square at impact. The sweet spot for most clubs is slightly off-centre towards the heel of the club. The club must be swung with the clubface square, along the target line. This is the correct path.

The clubhead moving downwards is the angle of attack that will produce the best shots with the irons and fairway woods. However, the driver should be hit slightly on the upswing.

The Grip

There are three basic grips you can use: the overlapping or Vardon grip, the interlocking grip and the baseball grip.

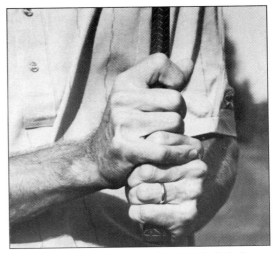

In the overlapping grip or Vardon grip, the little finger of the right hand overlaps the forefinger of the left hand.

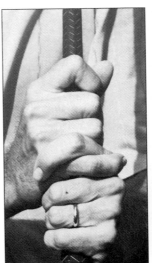

In the interlocking grip, the little finger of the right hand interlocks with the forefinger of the left hand.

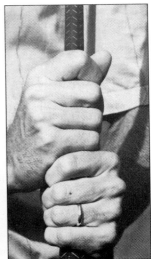

In the baseball grip, all the fingers of both hands are on the shaft.

Checking your Grip

Check to see that your hands work together as one unit. Use a greater grip pressure in the last three fingers of the left hand and the two middle fingers of the right hand. This should prevent loosening of the grip at the top of the backswing.

Check the Vs of your grip. The left V should point to the chin and the right V to the right shoulder. Keep the hands high and square throughout the swing with no tilt from side to side or up and down. Keep the body still and steady for a good shot.

The grip must be correct, since no golf shot can be accurate unless the grip is correct to begin with. The next important thing is to have the address correct at the beginning. If both the grip and the address are right, then the backswing, downswing, impact and followthrough are much easier.

The Drive

When you are perfecting your ultimate golf swing, you need to break down the stance and movement into sections: the address; the backswing; the downswing; and the followthrough.

The Address for the Drive

1   Place the ball 1 in/2.5 cm back from the target heel.

2   Assume a slightly closed stance, keeping the heels shoulder-width apart. The weight should be slightly on the right foot.

3   Turn the left toe-cap one-quarter turn to the left.

4   Straighten the right foot, or turn it one-eighth turn to the right.

5   Flex the knees.

6 Keep the elbows close together.

7 Keep the arms straight but not rigid. Keep the right arm soft. Straighten the left arm.

8 Keep the hands slightly behind the ball.

9 Square the body to the target line and stay comfortably erect.

10 Bend forwards from the hips until the weight is on the balls of the feet.

11 Take the proper grip.

12 Tap the heels so that the legs feel alive.

13 Relax and swing in balance.

The Angle of the Back at the Address

1 Remember that the angle of the back in the address position is important and it should remain the same throughout the swing.

2 Do not change the angle from side to side or up and down.

3 Keep your back in the same angle, turning around the spine, throughout the entire swing.

4 The body position at impact should always be about the same as it was at the address.

The Backswing for the Drive

1 Move the triangle of the shoulders, arms and hands, co-ordinated with the hips, straight back from the ball and past the right foot.

2 Continue upwards to a full backswing. The wrists will cock naturally above the head. The shoulders will turn fully and the back will be towards the target. The hips also turn.

3 Point the club over your right shoulder towards the target. The club may be taken back to horizontal if that position is comfortable and you are able to manage the club.

The Downswing for the Drive

The Half-followthrough with the Driver

1 Start the downswing by turning the left hip to the left, which causes the target heel to lower and the weight to begin to transfer to the target leg. This also drops the triangle towards the waist and the rear foot, as the arms and hands move into the hitting area below the waist. The left arm will be guiding, and the right hand ready to smash the ball.

2 The swing is down and through the ball.

3 The clubhead contacts the ball slightly on the upswing, sweeping the ball off the tee. The body stays steady throughout the swing, so the body position at impact is about the same as it was at the address.

1 Continue the swing through impact and out towards the target, the right arm now straightening and the left arm folding into a natural, high followthrough, completely in balance. The swing has been done around a steady spine. The address posture stays the same throughout the swing.

2 As you move through the downswing, the right shoulder moves down and under as the triangle moves through the impact and followthrough.

Target Golf

Concentrate on playing 'target' golf. Hit to a spot you have visualised. Just set up, waggle and swing! By this time your swing, timing, tempo and rhythm should be grooved, so I recommend that practice swings be eliminated when you play golf. The time to groove your swing is on the practice green or on the driving range, not on the course. The elimination of practice swings will improve your shots and your confidence. Your play will be quicker, with no wasted motion, and the game will be much more enjoyable.

The following is the recommended swing length for:

- **Chip shots:** Take the club back one-eighth of a swing.
- **Short pitch shots:** Take the club back one-quarter of a swing.
- **Pitch shots:** Take the club back one-half of a swing.
- **Short iron shots:** Take the club back three-quarters of a swing.
- **Middle iron shots:** Take the club back three-quarters of a swing.
- **Long iron shots:** Take the club back three-quarters of a swing.
- **Fairway woods:** Take the club back shoulder-high.
- **Tee shots (driver):** Take the club back head-high.

These swing lengths will provide the best control of the club and the least wear and tear on the back.

Bunkers

I have previously recommended that you use pitch shots from bunkers. The following is advanced information on how to hit shots from the sand with the sand wedge.

The Explosion Shot

1 Assume a slightly open stance.

2 Keep the feet shoulder-width apart.

3 Keep the feet dug into the sand for a firm footing.

4 Place the ball 1 in/2.5 cm back from target heel.

5 Break the wrists quickly on the backswing.

6 Allow the hands to lead the clubhead in the downswing.

7 Use a firm grip pressure.

8 Keep the clubface slightly open.

9 Hit 2 in/5 cm behind the ball.

10 Keep the head still.

11 Follow through, and finish with the left palm downwards to keep the face open during the swing.

The power of the swing will determine the distance, and the object in sand shots is to put the ball near the hole. The texture of the sand also influences distance. Wet or coarse sand will help distance, but dry, powdery sand is hard to escape from and requires a full explosion shot.

The 'fried egg' lie requires a firm downward swing. Strike the sand 2 in/5 cm behind the ball. Place the ball in line with the rear heel. The club will dig into the sand to lift the ball out of the trap.

The Stance for the Explosion Shot from the Sand with the Sand Wedge

1 Assume a slightly open stance. Feet are shoulder-width apart.

2 Dig the feet into the sand for a firm footing.

3 Place the ball 1 in/2.5 cm back from the target heel.

4 Use a firm grip pressure.

5 Open the clubface slightly.

6 Hit 2 in/5 cm behind the ball.

7 Keep the head still.

One-quarter Backswing with the Sand Wedge

1 Break the wrists quickly on the backswing.

2 Keep the clubface open during the swing.

Full Backswing with the Sand Wedge

1 In the full backswing, the club is taken to shoulder height.

2 Determine the distance you need to put the ball near the hole and adjust the power of the swing accordingly.

3 Remember that the texture of the sand also influences distance.

One-half Downswing with the Sand Wedge

1 Lead the clubhead in the downswing with the hands.

2 The body turns around a steady spine.

Impact with the Sand Wedge

1   The hit is down and through the sand and ball.

2   The left arm is guiding, and the right arm is ready to smash the ball.

One-quarter Followthrough with the Sand Wedge

1   Move the triangle through impact into the one-quarter followthrough position.

One-half Followthrough with the Sand Wedge

Full Followthrough with the Sand Wedge

1   Do not move the head from its starting position.

2   The swing should remain in perfect balance.

1   Finish with the left palm downwards to keep the clubface open during the swing.

Uneven Lies in the Sand

Uphill Lie

Position yourself so that the ball is opposite your right toe. Your weight should be on your rear foot. Take an open stance, with feet, hips and shoulders aligned to the left of the target and hit 1 in/2.5 cm behind the ball.

Downhill Lie

Place the ball so it is opposite the rear heel, with the weight on the target foot, for a downhill lie. Hit 2½ in/6 cm behind the ball and keep your follow-through short.

Chip from the Sand

Hit this type of shot when you have a clean lie. Set up as for a regular chip shot, and play the ball near the rear foot. Your weight should be mostly on your target foot. Hit down and through the ball, striking the ball before you strike the sand.

From Fairway Traps

Be sure to choose a club to produce a shot that will clear the lip. Anchor your feet and make a normal swing. Be sure to contact the ball first, before the sand.

Maintaining the Same Address Routine for All Shots

For each shot you make, first stand behind the ball, then note the line and the shot trajectory and locate the target. Select a club for the shot and ground the clubface square to your target on the fairway. Imagine a line from the target to the ball. This is the 'target line'. Then imagine a line from the ball through the feet. This is the 'ball line'. Put your feet in the proper position, with the target foot slightly to the left and the rear foot at the proper angle. Sight the target again and hold the image in your mind. Waggle and swing!

Make sure that your clubs are clean, the grips are good and your equipment is in good repair. A well-ordered routine to maintain your equipment will not only add much to your golfing pleasure, but will result in lower scores.

When Hitting All Clubs

When the clubhead enters the impact area on any swing, the weight will shift to the target foot, allowing a hit 'through the ball', with a smash of force towards the target. By halfway through the finish of a swing, the arms should be fully extended and the body posture of the address preserved. When a swing is completed, most of the weight will be on the target foot, and the rear heel will be off the ground. The hands should finish high, with the posture in balance. The body will be facing the target. Allow the angle of the clubface to do the work in lifting the ball from the ground.

The Address for all Clubs

1   Hold the last three fingers of the left hand firmly on the club to prevent a loose grip during the swing.

2   Relax and always keep the head still.

The Backswing for all Clubs

1   Use the full or three-quarter backswing, maintaining your style and posture.

The Followthrough for all Clubs

1 Allow the angle of the clubface to do the work in lifting the ball from the ground.

2 Shift the weight to the target foot when the clubhead enters the impact area, allowing a hit through the ball, with a smash of force towards the target.

3 Fully extend the arms halfway through the finish and preserve the body posture of the address.

4 Transfer most of the weight to the target foot when the swing is completed. The rear heel will be off the ground.

5 Finish high with the hands as the posture stays in balance. The body faces the target at the finish.

Hitting a Deliberate Slice

The left-to-right slice is used to play around trees or other obstacles. The address for the deliberate slice is as follows:

1 Assume an open stance.

2 Align the open stance to the left of the target line.

3 Aim the clubhead at the target.

4 Place the ball just ahead of the centre of the stance.

5 Swing down the target line.

The swing will be slightly shortened. The ball will be contacted first at impact, before turf is taken. The slightly open clubface will impart a slice to the ball.

Hitting a Deliberate Hook

The right-to-left hook shot may also be used to play around trees, bushes and other obstacles. The address for the deliberate hook is as follows:

1 Assume a closed stance.

2 Align the stance to the right of the target line.

3 Aim the clubhead at the target.

4 Place the ball between the left heel and the centre of the stance.

5 Swing the club down the target line.

The swing will be slightly shortened. The ball will be contacted first on impact, before taking turf. The slightly closed clubface imparts a hook to the ball.

CHAPTER 6

SHOTS FOR PLAYING GOLF

Frequently Used Golf Shots

The following is a guide to some of the most frequently used golf shots, along with some strategies for handling special situations you might encounter.

How to Fade

This is a gentle left-to-right shot. Set up comfortably in a slightly open stance. Aim the clubface at the target and swing down the target line.

How to Draw

This is a gentle right-to-left shot. Set up comfortably in a slightly closed stance. Aim the clubface at the target and swing down the target line.

How to Hit the Soft Fade

Address the ball with a slightly open stance with hips and shoulders turned slightly to the left. Aim the clubface at the target. Play the ball near the left heel. Do not let the right hand cross the left until well past impact. Swing down the target line.

How to Hit the Punch Shot

This shot will fly low and is useful against a strong breeze. Set up comfortably, with the weight on the left leg. Shorten the grip 3 in/7.5 cm. Hit down sharply on impact. Contact the ball solidly.

How to Hit the Cut Shot

This short shot is hit from the fairway or from traps around the green and will fly high, stopping quickly. Set up with an open stance. Open the clubface and play the ball opposite the target heel. Let the wrists cock fully.

How to Hook

This is a strong right-to-left shot. Assume a closed stance and play the ball further back than you normally would. Grip to the right, with the left hand on top. Vs point to the outside of the right shoulder. Flatten the swing.

How to Slice

This is a strong left-to-right shot. Assume an open stance. Play the ball more forward than you would normally. The grip is to the left and the Vs point at the chin. Take the club straight back. Retain left-hand dominance.

How to Hit a High Shot

Play the ball forwards, opening the clubface slightly as you do so. The hands are positioned over the clubhead. Hit the ball at the low point of the swing. Increase the wrist action and put more weight on the right foot.

How to Hit the Low Shot

Play the ball further back, closing the clubface slightly. Use a shorter, stiff-wristed swing. Have more weight on the target foot and hit down and through.

On the Green

Rolling Green

Bear in mind that slopes nearer the hole will change the direction of the ball more, because slopes have more effect as the ball slows down.

Depressed Green

Approach more boldly, but try for position on the low side of the hole, since a depressed green will tend to make the ball pull up short.

Elevated Green

Approach less boldly, since the ball will have a tendency to run. Pitch high for maximum bite, to stop the ball on the green.

Wet Green

Stroke the ball more firmly, because putts won't break as far when the green is wet. Move the ball if casual water impedes the course to the cup.

Difficult Lies

Uphill Lie

Use one less lofted club and aim slightly to the right. Play the ball forwards. Bend the target knee. Use a low backswing and a straight followthrough.

Downhill Lie

Use one more lofted club and aim slightly to the left. Play the ball further back. Bend the rear knee. Stay down over the shot.

Sidehill Lie with the Ball Above the Feet

Use one less lofted club. Shorten the grip, open the stance and keep the weight on the balls of the feet. Aim slightly to the right. Maintain a straight followthrough.

Sidehill Lie with the Ball Below the Feet

Use one less lofted club. Stand closer and set down to the shot with the weight on the heels. Keep the hands forward and aim slightly to the left. Stay down over the shot.

Close Lie

Play the ball back slightly. Keep the weight on the target leg. Hit down and through and don't try to scoop. Let the loft of the clubface do the lifting.

Heavy Rough

Sacrifice distance to get safely out of the rough. Play the ball centred between the legs. Have a firm grip and a more upright swing. Hit down and through. Contact the ball first and don't scoop.

Bunkers

Hard Wet Sand

Putt or chip the ball if possible. Contact the ball first or use the explosion shot. Use a firmer grip and don't dig as deeply. Follow through.

Explosion Shot

Open the stance and keep the clubface open. Plant the feet firmly. Play the ball off the target heel. Keep the hands forward. Make a three-quarter swing, with a full wrist cock. The clubface should enter the sand 2 in/5 cm behind the ball. Follow through.

Ball Embedded in Sand

Play the ball back, with the hands ahead of the clubhead. Square your stance and close the clubface. Make your swing more upright and hit more firmly, taking less sand than in the explosion shot.

Long Bunker Shots

Use a more lofted club than you normally would for the same distance. Plant the feet firmly. Play the ball centred between the legs, with the weight on the target heel. Shorten the grip and shorten the swing. Contact the ball first and pick it clean.

Special Shots

Water Hazard

Open the stance and keep the clubface open. Use a firmer grip than normal. Enter water well behind the ball. Be sure to contact the ball before hitting bottom. This is only to be attempted by the very confident!

Cross Wind

Use one less lofted club than you normally would for the same distance. Tee the ball on the side from which the wind is blowing and play that side of the fairway.

Shallow Trap Shots

Putt out, if the trap has no lip. If there is a low lip, chip with a club two numbers higher than usual. Contact the ball first and don't scoop.

Stopping the Ball with the Pitching Wedge

Take a slightly open stance with the feet about 10 in/ 25 cm apart. Grip down about 1 in/2.5 cm and play the ball off the target heel. Keep your eyes on the ball and strike the ball sharply as the clubhead moves through the ball. The shot should be smooth and crisp. The result is a backspin that will stop the ball on the green.

The iron clubface for this shot must be clean, with no dirt or grass to clog the grooves. The grooves impart a backspin to the ball when the club is swung downwards through impact, contacting the ball before taking turf.

Wet Weather Golf

When the weather is wet, play with a slightly wider stance. Keep both feet on the ground when hitting clubs from the short irons through the middle irons. Lift the heel slightly on long iron and fairway wood shots. Pick the ball clean and don't hit behind the ball, because the shot will be ruined and mud will fly.

Try to stay dry as much as you can. Use an umbrella. If possible, wear a rain suit and golf overshoes. Wear a waterproof hat. Take along an extra glove. Keep the glove and the grips of the clubs dry. On the green, hit putts firmly to make certain that they roll to the hole.

Swing slower and more deliberately. Make solid contact with the ball and expect to lose some distance. Allow for this loss with a planning strategy for playing wet weather golf.

Dry and clean the clubs after a wet round. Dry the bag, the wood covers and your other equipment.

Wet Fairway

Hit the ball first, not the turf behind it. Pick the ball off the grass cleanly and try to keep the ball in the air as long as possible. Approach more boldly, pitching rather than chipping.

CHAPTER 7
PREPARATION AND STRATEGY

There are a number of things you can do to improve your game, including physical exercises and concentrating on your mental attitude.

Exercises

Regular targeted exercises can help to improve both flexibility and style.

Exercise 1
Swing a 22 oz/550 g training club to strengthen golf muscles and to help groove a swing.

Exercise 2
Assume the address position without a club. Swing the arms and hands to the top of the backswing. Check that the left knee bends in behind an imaginary ball position, and then swing through impact to a full followthrough. Check to see that the weight transfers to the target leg and the right knee points behind the imaginary ball. Turn around a stationary spine. Keep the head still and swing backwards and forwards until you do this ten times.

Exercise 3
Assume the address position facing a wall, bend forwards and place a small cushion between your forehead and the wall. Swing backwards and forwards into the backswing and the downswing. Keep pressure on the cushion and turn around a steady spine.

Exercise 4
Grasp a rolled-up towel at each end. Assume the address position and swing the arms through the backswing and downswing. Release the right hand and snap the towel with the left hand in the followthrough.

Exercise 5
Assume the address position and stretch the arms out straight. Place the right wrist behind the left and apply resisting pressure with the back of the left hand until you can reach the top of the backswing. Reverse the hands and repeat in the downswing.

Exercise 6
Grasp an iron club at the ends. Place the right hand under and the left hand over in the address position, then make a full swing.

Exercise 7
Assume the address position and grasp the left arm above the left wrist. Swing to the top of the backswing with the thumb extended in a hitchhiker position. Swing through downswing to followthrough with the left thumb in the hitchhiker position.

Exercise 8

Lie flat on the floor with the feet together. Then raise one leg and swing it over and up and return it to the floor position. Repeat with the other leg. Be careful to keep the back flat when you swing the legs. Repeat at least ten times for each leg.

Exercise 9

Stand at attention with the arms at the sides, then raise the arms above the head and swing them in rotation around the shoulders. Repeat at least ten times.

The Address Position Drill

1   Stand with the back against a wall with the feet shoulder-width apart.

2   Place both heels 3 in/7.5 cm from the wall. Point your right foot straight ahead and point your left foot one-quarter to the left.

3   Place the back square against the wall with the head touching the wall.

4   Flex the knees so that the body slides 1 in/2.5 cm down the wall.

5   Bend forwards from the hips so that the weight moves to the balls of the feet.

6   Let the arms hang free and lower the right shoulder so that the right hand can move below the left in the gripping position inside the left knee.

7   Tap the heels to make sure you are properly balanced.

Side view of the address position drill.

Front view of the address position drill.

The Warm-up

The purpose of warming up before playing a round of golf is to stretch and loosen the muscles used in the swing. Do a few warm-up exercises before taking some practice shots.

Warm-up Exercises

1   Grasp a club at each end and hold it in front of the body. Raise it above the head and lower it behind the back. Extend both arms.

2   Hold a club behind the back in the elbow joints. Turn the body around the spine but keep the feet stationary. Turn back and forth.

Warm-up Shots

Thirty to forty shots are enough. Start with the short irons, then move on to the middle irons, the long irons, the fairway woods and then the tee shots. Finish up with chip shots, short pitch shots, pitch shots and putts.

Check your swing tendencies, tempo and timing. This should clue you in on the pattern of shots you can expect in the coming round of golf. In the first stages of the warm-up, think about your swing. In the last part of the warm-up, think of the golf you are going to play.

Begin by making a few shots with your feet together. Try to make solid contact with the ball. Develop good rhythm and wait for the clubhead to come into the hitting area, through impact and into the followthrough. After this, return to normal shots. If you are short of time and can't hit practice shots, warm up by swinging three clubs together. This will loosen stiff muscles.

If you are right-handed, take several swings from the left side (from the right side for left-handed players). Finish by taking slow backswings and downswings and easy followthroughs.

When you come to the first tee, remember to swing easily and accelerate through the ball. Relax on all your shots. Tense muscles cannot swing a golf club correctly. Hit a few practice putts before you start if possible.

Concentration

Close mental application and/or exclusive attention must be used in managing and executing a golf shot. Golf is a relaxing game, and the walk between holes is to be enjoyed. However, when it is your turn to hit, the pre-shot routine is vital. The short time used in the pre-shot routine is the player's concentration time. This routine must be repeated precisely on every golf shot. Here is my recommended pre-shot routine.

1   Stand behind the ball and look down the target line. Locate an intermediate spot for the shot to travel over.

2   Ground the clubhead with the clubface square to that spot on the target line.

3   Imagine a line from the ball to the feet opposite the target line.

4   Move the left foot a short distance towards the target, then move the right foot into position.

5   Sight the target again, waggle and swing.

Concentrate on each part of the pre-shot routine. Don't let yourself be distracted. As you look down the fairway, visualise the shot and where it will land. Every player would do well to practise visualisation on every shot he or she makes until it is second nature. This process must take place in practice as well as when playing the course. The pre-shot routine is similar to that of tennis, bowling or basketball.

The Mental Part of Golf

Learning to control emotions on a golf course is vital to improving golf scores. Losing one's temper and tightening up will ruin a golf shot. Recovery from fear, nervousness and tension is a part of the game that must be learned if progress towards lower golf scores is to be made.

Every golfer experiences anxiety to some extent in making a shot, but the good golfer learns to control it. Learn to develop a competitive edge. Learn to relax. Increase your powers of visualisation and develop a strategic plan for the round you plan to play. Don't respond to pressure. Don't let a bad round create negative feelings. All players experience a bad round occasionally. Think positive and build success in playing golf.

On-course Strategy

Plan to play well. This is no time to practise. This is the time to shoot the best score possible. This is the way to keep your swing in tune and your score improving.

There are times when a normal shot cannot be made. This is no time to gamble. Make the safe shot which will take the ball back to the fairway. On the fairway, be a hero and hit the next shot to the pin.

Always hit short of a hazard if you have any doubt about clearing it. It is better to be safe than sorry you have missed a shot. Know the rules; they will save you many strokes. Speed up your game by planning your stance while approaching the ball. Set up square to the target.

When pressure builds, don't tighten up. If you are the underdog, play well and believe that you can beat your opponent. Play competitively only when handicaps are honest.

Leave the driver in the bag when the fairway is tight and the shot calls for accuracy. Always count your clubs before you start a round of golf.

Off-course Strategy

Keep records for analysis of your game and your progress. Record such things as the following:

1   The number of fairways hit or missed off the tee.

2   The number of greens you hit in regulation figures. Regulation figures are two shots less than par for the hole. Here are some examples: A par 3 hole should have the ball on the green in one stroke. A par 4 hole should have the ball on the green in two strokes. A par 5 hole should have the ball on the green in three strokes.

3   The number of putts on each hole.

4   The length of the putts for one round should be added together. Then divide the total by the number of putts. The result will be the average length of the putts you have sunk in that round.

5   The number of times you have got down from off the green in two shots.

CHAPTER 8
TROUBLESHOOTING

Problem	Cause	Correction
Lack of distance	Hitting from the top or uncocking the wrists prematurely	Lead with the hips on the downswing, with the arms and hands following in one piece
Scooping	Trying to 'lift' the ball by hitting it on the upswing	Keep the hands forward and the weight on the target leg. Hit the ball before taking a divot. Let the club lift the ball for you.
Difficulty starting back	Lack of preliminary movements	Waggle, sole the club, press forwards, then take the club back in one piece.
Picking up the clubhead	Right-hand dominance	Grip more firmly with the left hand. Start back low, all in one piece, and lead with the hips.
Falling forwards	Poor distribution of weight	Bend the knees and 'sit down' to the ball. Keep the weight more on the heels.
Moving target foot	Lifting the target heel too high on the backswing	Lift the heel only as much as necessary to make the proper pivot.
Falling backwards	Poor transfer of weight	Shift the weight to the rear foot on the backswing, so it can flow left on the downswing.
Swaying	Moving the body or head from side to side	Coil the body with the head steady.

Problem	Cause	Correction
Pushed putts	Placing the hands too far in front of the clubhead	Keep the hands slightly ahead of the clubhead at impact. The right hand should face the target.
Pulled putts	Closing the clubface after impact	Keep the clubface square throughout the stroke.
Lack of backspin	Trying to 'lift' or 'scoop' the ball	Hit the ball first, then take the divot. Let the clubface do the lifting. Hit down and through.
Unable to get out of a trap	Taking too much sand or quitting on the shot	Look at a spot 1–2 in/2.5–5 cm behind the ball. This is where the club should enter the sand. Follow through.
Skying	Hitting the ball below the centre; chopping the downswing; right-hand dominance; or having too much weight on the target leg at impact	Start back low, all in one piece. Transfer the weight to the right so it can shift back to the left on the downswing. Keep the left hand firm at the top. Start down with the hips leading and retain the arm and hand action as long as possible. Do not sway.
Pulling the ball straight left of the target	Keeping the clubface closed to the direction line, square to the outside-in swing; throwing the club from the top or right hand overpowers the left	Shift the weight to the rear leg on the backswing. Make a 45 degree hip pivot. Keep the head fixed with no sway at the top, and the left hand firm. Point the clubhead at the target and start down in one piece, hips leading. Shift the weight to the target foot. The arms and hands should follow inside the ball's projected line of flight.

Problem	Cause	Correction
Hooking the ball left of the target	Keeping the clubface closed to the direction line and the path of the swing; gripping too far around to the right; a flat swing with rolling wrists; or right hand overpowers the left on the downswing	Adjust your grip to the left until the first three knuckles of the left hand are visible. The Vs should point to the inside of the right shoulder. Start the backswing all in one piece. Let the left arm dominate and keep the left hand firm at the top. Start down, all in one piece, with the hips leading and the wrists cocked.
Smothering, so the ball never gets off the ground	The right hand is overpowering the left to the point that the clubface is hooded at impact, which eliminates its built-in loft	Adjust the grip to the left, with three knuckles of the left hand visible. The Vs should point to the inside of the right shoulder. Keep the left hand firm at the top. Lead the downswing with the hips, while the hands and arms follow in one piece.
Topping – hitting above the centre of the ball	Straightening up, swaying or otherwise changing the arc of the the swing; having the weight on the rear leg at impact, which moves the swing backwards	Don't bend too far over or reach for the ball. Stand more erectly. Transfer the weight to the rear leg on the backswing so it can shift to the left in the downswing. Retain the hand and arm action as long as possible.
Scuffing – hitting the ground behind the ball	Having the weight on the rear leg at impact, or by trying to 'scoop', which throws the clubhead from the top into a chopping downswing	Start the backswing all in one piece, with the head fixed. Let the left arm dominate. Transfer the weight to the rear foot on the backswing so it can shift to the target leg in the downswing. Retain the arm and hand motion as long as possible.
Pulled or pushed chips	Opening the clubface on the backswing and closing on the followthrough	Take a shorter backswing, with firmer wrists and a straight followthrough.

Problem	Cause	Correction
Shanking – the ball scoots to the right off the neck of the club	Standing too close to the ball; a restricted pivot or an outside-in swing, which throws the clubhead behind the target line and causes the neck of the club to hit the ball	Stand 6 in/15 cm from the clubshaft. Start back all in one piece, with the left arm dominating. Make a 45 degree hip pivot. Point the club at the target and concentrate on a correct, smooth stroke.
Pushing the ball to the right of the target	Opening the clubface to the target line; or a square to inside-out swing	Position yourself with the ball more forward, so the clubface will have time to square itself at impact. Start the backswing all in one piece and don't flatten the swing. Lead with the hips and don't sway.
Slicing – the ball curves to right of the target	Opening the clubface to the direction line and path of the swing, approaching the ball from the outside-in swing	Adjust the grip to the right so that the first three knuckles of the left hand are visible. The Vs should point at the right shoulder. Start back all in one piece, with no sway. At the top, keep the left hand secure. Point the club at the target and lead the downswing with the hips; the arms and hands all in one piece.
Fading – the ball starts out straight but picks up a tail-end slice	Opening the clubface to the direction line and the path of the swing or by gripping too far around to the left	Adjust the grip so that the first three knuckles of the left hand are visible. The Vs should point to the right shoulder. At impact, the clubface should be square to the target line and slightly closed to the inside-out swing.

CHAPTER 9
TERMINOLOGY

The following are some of the most commonly used terms in general use in golf today:

Address: Taking the correct stance, flexing the knees and bending from the hips. Aligning the club from behind the ball to the target. Checking the correct grip pressure and preparation for the swing.

Advice: Any counsel or suggestion that could influence a player in determining their play, their choice of club or their method of making a stroke.

Air shot: Missing the ball completely.

Angle of attack: The level angle at which the club moves into the ball.

Approach: A shot to the green.

Apron: Closely mown grass around the green.

Away: Ball furthest from the hole to be played first.

Ball deemed to move: If the ball leaves its position and comes to rest in another lie, it is 'deemed to move'.

Ball holed: The ball is holed when it lies in the hole.

Ball lost: If the ball cannot be found within five minutes, it is declared lost by the player, or if after five minutes the player is unable to identify a ball as their ball, the ball is considered to be lost.

Bent: A type of grass used on greens and tee surfaces.

Best ball: A match in which one plays against the better ball of two players or the best ball of three players.

Birdie: One stroke under par for a hole.

Bogey competition: Stroke play in which golfers play against a fixed score at each hole of a stipulated round or rounds.

Bunker: A sand trap.

Bye: Unplayed holes after a match is won.

Casual water: Temporary accumulation of water. This is not a hazard.

Clubhead facing: The square angle the club should be facing at impact.

Clubhead path: The path on which the clubhead is moving at impact.

Clubhead speed: The force applied to the ball at impact.

Dead: A ball so close to the hole that there can be no doubt that the next stroke will sink it.

Divot: Turf removed by a player's club when swung properly.

Dogleg: A hole that curves right or left to reach the green.

Dormie: When a player or side is as many holes up as there are holes left to play.

Down: In match play, the number of holes a player is behind. In stroke play, the number of strokes a player is behind.

Draw: A shot that curves from the right to the left.

Drop: Take relief from an unplayable hole.

Eagle: Two strokes under par for a hole.

Fade: A shot that curves from the left to the right.

Fairway: The route of play from tee to green.

Flagstick: A moveable pole with a flag placed in the hole to show its location. Also called a pin.

Fore: A yell to warn any player in the way of a shot, errant or otherwise.

Four ball: A match in which one plays against the better ball of two or the best ball of three players, or two pairs playing each other with best score by each side to count on each hole.

Foursome: Two players against two, with each side playing one ball.

Green: The putting surface.

Ground the club: Touching the sole of the club to the ground at the address.

Ground under repair: Any portion of the course so marked. It includes piled material and holes made by the greenskeeper.

Halved: Players having the same score on a hole in match play.

Handicap: Strokes allowed to be deducted from par. A player's handicap is computed by the proper handicap system.

Hazard: Water areas and bunkers.

Hole: A round receptacle in the green, $4\frac{1}{4}$ in/ 10.5 cm in diameter and 4 in/10 cm deep. Units of play from tee to green. A round consists of 18 holes.

Hole out: Putting the ball into the hole.

Honour: The player with the lowest score on the preceding hole tees off first.

Hook: The ball curves to the left of the target for right-handed players. The ball curves to the right of the target for left-handed players.

Hosel: Extension of the clubhead into which the shaft fits.

Lie: Position of the ball in the grass or sand. Also the angle of the clubshaft to the ground when soled.

Loose impediment: A leaf, twig or natural object adhering to the ball. You can move it, as long as this does not move your ball at all.

Marker: A scorekeeper. Also markers showing limits of the tee-off area on a hole to be played, known as tee boxes or pegs.

Marker (ball): Small coin or plastic marker used to mark the ball location on the green when the ball is moved.

Match: A contest between two or more players.

Match play: In which each hole is decided by better nett score. The player who wins the most holes wins the match, after discounting those 'halved'.

Medal play: Competition in which results are determined by the number of strokes played. Essentially, each player plays the course, not each other.

Nassau: Players competing in match play or stroke play. The winner is awarded one point for the first 9, one point for the back 9 and one point for 18 holes.

Net score: The total score less the player's handicap.

Obstruction: An object erected or placed on the course.

Out of bounds: Ground on which play is prohibited.

Par: Playing the hole in the number of strokes listed on the card for the hole.

Penalty: A stroke or strokes added to the score of a player or side under certain rules, such as hitting out of bounds, taking relief when the ball is unplayable.

Preferred lie: See 'Winter rules'.

Provisional ball: A second ball hit if the first ball appears to be lost, out of bounds or in a water hazard.

Pull: A straight shot which flies left of the target.

Push: A straight shot which flies right of the target.

Putt: Playing a stroke on the green.

Putting green: Ground prepared for putting. All ground around the hole.

Relief: Dropping the ball in prescribed fashion after retrieving it from an unplayable lie.

Rough: Long grass close to the tee, fairway, hazards or greens.

Rub of the green: A condition arising when a ball in motion is stopped or deflected by an agency outside the match.

Sand save: Par 3 holes: a shot from the sand that can be holed in one stroke. Par 4 holes: two putts. Par 5 holes: three putts.

Slice: A shot which curves to the right for a right-handed player or to the left for a left-handed player.

Sole: Act of placing the clubhead on the ground at the address.

Square: A match that is even in holes won or lost.

Stance: The position of the feet when addressing the ball.

Stroke: The forward motion of the club to impact the ball.

Stroke play: Competition based on the total number of strokes played. Same as medal play.

Target: The spot where the ball is expected to land.

Tee: The peg on which the ball is placed on the tee before striking the ball.

Tee box: Defines the area of the tee currently in use.

Teeing ground: The area from which the play on each hole starts.

Three ball: A match in which three play against one another, each playing his or her own ball.

Threesome: A match in which one plays against two and each side plays one ball.

Top: A ball hit above its centre.

Twosome or Two ball: One player playing against another.

Up: The number of holes by which a player leads their opponent in match play.

Waggle: Preliminary action, swinging the club backwards and forwards.

Whiff: Missing the ball entirely, also known as an 'air shot'.

Winter rules: Local club rule (not part of R & A rules) allowing the player to move the ball no more than 6 in/15 cm to a better lie, but not near the hole.

INDEX